Mirrored

Injustice

By

Cookie Johnson Grant

ISBN (Paperback): 979-8218566098

ISBN (Hardcover): 979-8218566104

Cookie Johnson Grant

Dedication

To My Mother, *Gloria A Johnson.*

Cookie Johnson Grant

Acknowledgment

I would like to thank my two Sons and Granddaughter for quiet time.

Cookie Johnson Grant

Preface

I am surrounded by Mirrors

I don't like these mirrors

I see one

I see two

I see three

Then I see me

If I stare long enough

I know the answers is within what I see

To ask myself how I feel

My mind becomes to jealous

To handle my soul

Getting to know betrayals

The eyes in the Mirrors

See all my sins

The mind controls the body

It's the body that say when

If I mend the skin

Moldings eventually take shape

Everything is fate

Cookie Johnson Grant

Force eyes and souls to become friends

Camouflage pain

Celebrate endurance

Add never subtract

Forward never back

Take advice

Born, live, die

Before you mirror yourself

Don't ask yourself why

CONTENTS

Cookie Johnson Grant

Mirrored Injustice

Craze mania swept the nation. News programs, Oprah, Geraldo, Russia Germany, Gorbachev, Cocaine, pot and unemployment swept the city like the plague. The year was 1988.

If you didn't owe I.R.S you were probably on welfare. You had your: extraterrestrials, telekinesis an let's not forget Starwars coming to life. That's if the atomic doesn't make the world meaningless.

Ronald Reagan leaving. LORD knows people was scared enough without having to think about who was next. Thinking was something most people avoided. Partying and partaking was priority, voting wasn't. If you voted it was fine. If you didn't that was fine too.

Grandparents and old people were wise. Their sayings that was passed down seemed somewhat eerie. Tia's Grandma used to always say to her that the only way you can tell the world is about to come to an end was when you could no longer tell the sexes apart. And at that point a horn would blow around the nation and everyone would hear it simultaneously.

She expected to hear a horn blow every time she went out. To her, the people in her town had no sex or identity. They were party mother-fuckers of the highest quality. She crossed her legs more to reach her toenails as she manicured them with her limber body discarding the nails onto the plush carpet in her Aspen Condo that overlooked the slopes and the map made streets.

Her parents had just sold their home in which she lived since birth. They celebrated by taking a trip to the South of France. Trusting her to be alone although she knew they didn't trust her at all.

She stood up stretching her five foot ten inch frame, tossing her thick dark mane out of her eyes. In her bedroom she looked at her canopy bunk beds wondering why her parents even after giving up the home which benefited them well after Tia's young adult years were gone. She wondered why they still thought she needed canopy bunk beds enough to request them to come with their newly decorated, rented Condo.

Dressing slowly in her full length Mirror she knew she was special. A full-fledged fox no doubt. Her hips attracted men long before her face came into focus. Her face was a stone rock carved to perfection.

Sometime she wondered how her mediocre looking folks produced her striking being. She was vane yet she strived to put the rich pretty girl image behind her, finally show her folks and that she could be responsible.

Grands Morgan was eighty-three kicking and lived in Aspen all her life.

To listen to her tell it, she inherited their grocery store which was now a market from her late husband she courted since elementary school.

Tia used to argue with Grand about how could she inherit something she worked for all her life. As she got

2

older she learned it was better to let Grands tell her story her way. Grands seemed to doubt her no matter what. She made it clear that Tia wasn't worthy enough for their dreams to prosper after her final exit. Tia knew Grands way of thinking and she benefited from her money, but she would die before she let it be known she didn't know what she would do without her.

She applied her makeup carefully. What a relief it was not to have her parents ragging her about the Cobra. Her Dad rented them this Condo until his architects could put together their perfect home to satisfy Mother, she knew there wasn't a contractor alive that could put together a house that would please her Mom.

The phone rang and broke her thoughts, she wobbled to the phone because her toenails were wet and her 501 jeans were too tight. Hello her voice cracked, she cleared her throat. Hello, she tried to sound her best praying with her eyes closed that it was the Cobra. Hi Tia. It's Grands. Oh hi Grands, what's up? Tia please don't what's up me, I guess prices taxes, and probably your breast. Grands laughed, coughed, and choked before she caught her breath. Listen little girl, get your butt over here, you're two hours late. Your Mother just called me from abroad. I lied to her and I told her you were here. In the toilet, so she's going to call back in fifteen minutes. Thanks for covering for me Grands but I can't make it tonight. Tia expected the crying trip but

3

she didn't expect silence. Grands said nothing. Ah come on Grands say something.

Still silence. O.K. I'll be there in about an hour, I'm not dressed yet. Which was the truth, I'm now hanging up. She put the phone down looking into the mirror at her perfect ten, wondering why she lied. She knew that she wouldn't see Grands tonight. She was out to party with the Cobra who was a well-known stripper from New York's finest. Now he was in the Rocky Mountains. She walked from the phone as it rang again. She stumbled almost breaking her toe. It was a wrong number.

One hour later she entered The Peeper. Her boots crossed the threshold as the men turned to look, their tongues leaking with lust. The women immediately started to check and fix their clothing looking for the closest mirror as if to say to themselves, do I look as good as her?

Probably not, but I came here with this man, and I'm leaving the same way. Tia looked at no one, her head never turned. The Peeper was a favorite spot of everyone's. Lots of space. The decor was red velvet. It had a softness to it that would make you feel as if you were floating.

Focusing on the dance floor where the music bumped the party people were suspended in a world that was only theirs. In reality they had no choice.

Mirrored Injustice

The music was so loud, they could not hear each other. They danced until the music stopped, then ran to their tables for conversation. The next record started immediately. Tia made her way to the bar, as Mac the bartender spotted her long before she reached him. Ever willing to devote all his energy and attention to her, He threw her, his sexiest smile. She flashed her whites. Hi Mac, has the Cobra made an appearance tonight?" Not that I saw, rumor has it he took off for New York this morning with the Chap Stick bimbo. What's your pleasure? I'll have a margarita, hold the salt. He winked, I'm available, will I do?

Please Mac, I'm in no mood tonight, don't fuck with me. She slammed the margarita down and exited as fast as she entered, looking at no one but everyone knew of her appearance.

She walked the Mall with her hands stuffed in the sable her Dad brought her the Christmas before. The cold didn't matter. Damn him she thought, where is he when she needed him the most. She needed him right now as she had this hunch of something bad about tonight, something awful. She decided to check Mountain Express.

Although it wasn't a place he would likely frequent. It wasn't nearly as classy as The Peeper. It was a hole in the wall covered with nice pictures, and good food. If the Cobra didn't want to be found, Mountain Express would be the place for him to hide from whoever was looking for him, they would never suspect that he would grace a place of this nature.

It was on the corner smack in the middle of town. Next door was the First County Bank that Tia had been employed at for a very short while, thanks to Grands Morgan who thought Tia should do something worthwhile besides ski and spend her father's money. Worthwhile or not the employment lasted only one week.

The aroma at Mountain express stung her as soon as she entered. She instantly thought of New Orleans because of the food being prepared in back. Tia's nose sensed aroma's that reminded her of certain places she'd been. There weren't too many places she hadn't smelt or seen thanks to her Dad.

She pounced up on a stool, grabbing another stool to hold her back pack, gloves, and whatever else she decided to shed. She twisted her butt on the stool side-to-side to get a better view of the place. The crowd waved to her from the far corner. They looked like the racers classic ski team she skied with earlier that day.

Really she didn't want to be bothered, once they made eye contact there was no way to avoid the invitation.

She jumped down from her stool grabbed her belongings and joined the crowd. Everyone scooted

6

around the booth to make room for her. Hi girl, didn't expect to see your ass after the work out we gave you today. Yeah right, Tia said, don't worry about me. I can handle anything. As I remember it anyway, I helped all your asses up today with powder covering your faces. And you're on the racing team and I'm not. Well excuse me, Greg said. I was only trying to make conversation. Don't Tia said looking around for the Cobra. Has anybody seen the Cobra? Nope, Greg said but we're going dancing later at the Pyrimid. Can your legs stand it? I dunno, maybe we'll just have to see, she said anxiously. I'm not sure what I'll do once I catch up with the Cobra. She turned to get a better look at who was in the booth behind them. She saw two men in business suits that stuck out like sore thumbs. There wasn't a store in Aspen that sold three piece suits for men. Nobody in the town was interested in them or dressed that way. She turned her head back to focus on the people who were in front of her when she heard the name that was only supposed to be known to her and the Cobra in these neck of the woods. His God given name. The only people alive that knew it was Tia and the Cobra's family. And his family was more than three thousand miles away in Italy. Her thoughts were interrupted are you coming to the Pyrimid? Greg asked. We're going to bring the house down tonight I know you will Greg but I might meet up with you all later,

7

okay? Come on people We're gonna bring the house down tonight. Come on people, let's shake a leg. We've got some boogieing to do. They all grabbed their belongings and exited Mountain Express leaving Tia alone in the booth with the check.

She didn't mind. She was very interested in the conversation coming from the booth behind her. When the crowd was out the door and out of sight she stretched her legs out and eased her body down giving the men in the suits behind her a sense of privacy so they could talk freely about Tony Ryckman.

She realized if she squinted hard enough straight ahead she could see the figures through the reflection in the sign that blinked the words Miller Lite. She could only see the figures when the light blinked on. That was good enough for her.

At first she listened and thought the men in the suits were speaking a foreign language. She spoke three different languages and still she had to listen hard enough to keep up with their New York Mumbo Jumbo. It was much faster than all the lingo she was used to. She squinted hard at the picture on the wall in front of her and she saw one figure raise his drink to his head, finish it, and signal the bartender. As the bartender filled their order and walked pass her booth she politely raised her finger for him to refill her drink. Silence surrounded the booth as the bartender came and went. The figures sitting back to back from her which she could make out through the neon picture said look homeboy, whatever is done is done, let's not harp on it, neither one of us can change anything. I say we catch the next plane.

The other man in the suit who she couldn't see that well said, it's not about harping man we didn't follow orders and now you want to cop out with the job half done. Cuz, you cry too much the other fellow said, we did the best that we could and I say we split, the only way our boss will know what happen to Tony Ryckman is if one of us tells him, let's just play it straight, lie like hell get paid and go on with our lives. If you say so man but what if he lives? That's not likely 'cuz these doctors up here only know how to cope with ski injuries, bullets are not their specialty and so what if he does, what's he gonna do? Come back to New York? I doubt it. Tia turned pale and her heart started beating faster. She wrung her hands together trying to heat the chill that shook her. If what she heard was correct the Cobra was either dead or dying. She heard no more as the figures in the picture on the wall became blurry and the two men in the suits walked by her and out the door. Her legs could not move but her brain made her head for the door. At first her intentions were to just feel the cold air so she could think but at the red light she realized that she was following the men in the suits with the New York accents.

9

She followed them to the highway and out of town. Thank god, they turned into the airport which was two miles straight on the highway. She was in no shape to drive. Her thoughts were ridged with denial her body numb. She watched the men enter the rent a car terminal. She parked and decided to follow them on foot which led her into the main terminal. She watched as they conversed with the ticket agent briefly then seated themselves in front of the window to wait for their Rocky Mountain commuter plane to land; unload and reload again. She took a seat as close to them as she did not know what she could accomplish by waiting for a plane that she wasn't boarding, meanwhile biting her manicure to death.

After five minutes of waiting the taller man got up and she watched him ask the ticket agent a question then he headed for the bathroom she assumed. Her eyes darted back to the other man that's then she spotted the briefcase between the seats. She then realized that they had not checked in any luggage and whatever the connection with them and the Cobra had, it has to be in that briefcase, if their trip to Aspen was so short that not even a toothbrush was needed.

The guy in the seat yawned, rested his head back. She surprised herself as she walked over to him dropped her backpack beside his chair and with it she retrieved the briefcase.

Mirrored Injustice

She did it all in one second flat watching the direction the taller guy entered a minute earlier. She ran out of the airport to her car searching in her backpack for her keys, shaking too much to find them, she checked her coat pocket and there they were. She tried the trunk key, her condo key before she found the right key. Her hands shaking so bad she laughed at herself thinking this reminded her of something that she'd seen on HBO. She backed the car out and turned her head to check traffic then straightened her wheels out and one more final glance at the terminal doorway stood the figures in the suits staring directly into her eyes, she sped away.

Meanwhile, many miles away sat Sister Tangela Mancini with her mind just as complicated as her uniform. She Knelt with rosary in hand and prayed. Holy Father forgive me for I have sinned. There has got to be a better way, Father, it seems like every time I kneel before you I've sinned. I can't go on. Am I paying for my heritage which 1 know nothing of. Help me. Sister Tangela was an orphan all her life. Not belonging to anyone didn't bother her as much as not knowing what nationality she was. She didn't fit into any category. Her skin was light with an oven brown tan, her hair long silk, yet thick, her eyes had the look of nowhere, they told nothing. She had been orphaned in the Catholic environment for as long as she could remember. She came to the school for orphans at the age of five long before it had its name. Before that she moved from Catholic Church to Catholic Church always in the hands of the good sisters, Mother Mary and four Sisters took in five orphaned girls twenty years ago. They created the school from scratch with hard work and sweat. The five orphans turned into five good Sisters that Mother Mary prided herself with. They had become hard working, moldings of her. They were up at give five a.m., every morning and over to the school for cleaning, laundry, and paperwork. Then the underprivileged children were fed a hardy breakfast of oatmeal or cream of wheat. Then eight hours of intense study from the Sisters with a half hour break for lunch.

At the age of eighteen, Mother Mary gave all five of her first orphans a choice. Here are your working papers and your Social Security numbers. These are your choices. Those who want to stay on as good Sisters shall undergo extensive study for the next three years at St. Joseph college of Philadelphia with proper grants provided. Not until then will you be worthy and qualified to return here for work making this your home. Not as my children but as my peers. Those of you who don't choose that option may continue to stay on here at our home which we created together but only until you reach the age of twentyone. Then you shall select the life of your choice. If you choose to further educate yourself, funding will be provided for you for four years but only from this state of Pennsylvania.

Those of you who have turned eighteen, I shall expect a written response within twenty-four hours. Those of you who will be turning eighteen after today I expect you to respond within twenty-four hours after the date of your birth. Sisters you are entering women hood. I credit myself with your intelligence. It's up to you and our Christ almighty that your destination be based on what is right for you. Good luck Sisters. God bless each of you. May he guide you and be with you in whatever destiny you choose.

Sister Tangela Mancini's choice was made for her long ago one year after she came to Mother Mary as a babe of five. At thirteen her body started a drastic change her mind didn't accept. She found it impossible adjusting to the womanly changes so she decided to cover it up. She thought what one couldn't see, one wouldn't deal with or think of. So she took what God had given her and in all modesty kept it covered.

She prayed, Father why does the river flow red? Why is the sky so blue? Why am I here? She received no answer. Mother Mary needed an answer from her as she had raised her well. Sister Tangela Mancini was a true Sister indeed. She prospered well, a lady of grace. Her shaping no longer mattered and the perfect teacher was molded after her schooling was over. She loved children.

She taught them well although she was a little bothered by Ethan Blackwell, he was the new boy, mother Mary took in to work off his community service ordered by a Judge. Mr. Blackwell was smart mouthed and disrespectful to her and he didn't follow orders, or do his duties. He teased her something awful when they were alone together, he nicknamed her Tandy. She reminded him over and over again that her name was Sister Tangela

Mancini and he was there to work and not to rename God's helpers. Secretly she adored the name Tandy. She felt a sense of Deja vu when he said it.

As if she was called that in another life. But when thoughts of that life entered her mind she prayed.

One day in the chapel while she prayed, thinking she was alone, Sister Bridget Johnson joined her and wiped her tears. Sister Tangela, why do you cry so often? Let your tears flow. Let Gods' water cleanse your soul.

If I hadn't seen you in this Chapel, I would have never known your sorrows were back again. Please Sister come with me. I shall enlighten you and give you strength to make you stronger. With that she led Sister Tangela Mancini by the elbow down a poorly hit corridor.

Sister Tangela Mancini's uncontrolled tears watered her face as Sister Bridget Johnson led her into her own quarters. Once inside, Sister Bridget Johnson removed Sister Tangela Mancini's headdress. A sign to show her trust between the two. Although the removal of garments was strictly forbidden in front of any species that wasn't acting medically on Mother Mary's orders.

Let your tears flow Sister. Whatever troubles you now, Mother Mary will never know of. Sister Bridget Johnson wiped Sister Tangela Mancini's tears removing her own headdress slowly. Another thing, the trust between the two that only they would know of. I must return to my quarters, I shan't burden you with my problems. Sister Tangela Mancini said raising upwards. Sister Bridget Johnson gently stopped her from getting up. Sister Tangela Mancini I must confess what I have witnessed that I believe is making you so sad. Although the two Sisters were brought to the home together many years ago and raised with the same amount of compassion and respect and had been together practically all their lives. They had never managed the true act of being Sisters due to their upbringing. They treated one another with the same emotion as total strangers. Sister Tangela Mancini, Sister Bridget Johnson said. I have watched your reactions for some time now. Are your tears due to the young boy Mother Mary has as our helper from God? I've seen your ways of avoiding him when Mother Mary gives you the daily roster.

15

Cookie Johnson Grant

Why is it Sister that you seem to cannot give the boy his daily orders? I just can't Sister Tangela Mancini told Sister Bridget Johnson. He talks to me often. Sister he has to talk to you to follow his duties. Wiping Sister Tangela Mancini's tears and pushing her thick hair out of her face. You don't respond to his childlike boyish charm do you? No, but he won't stop, I never respond. He questions me and suggests things such as I'm not faithful to the church. He said he likes me. Sometime he tries to touch me. He tries to make me laugh. I can't laugh with a male Sister Bridget Johnson, can I?

Sister Bridget Johnson won the trust that sent her seeking. Please Sister Tangela Mancini, confide in me. What else are you to do?

With that Sister Bridget Johnson patted Sister Tangela Mancini's arm. My good Sister I'm going to relieve myself of some of these garments. It's awfully hot in here. Please Sister trust me enough to relieve yourself of some of those restricting garments.

Everything we do tonight is in the strictest of confidence. Please get comfortable. Let's talk this out. If we never confess to Mother Mary that we've unrobed this far. I will never repeat a word; what you trust in me tonight. With that she removed her clothing and gently started to massage Sister Tangela Mancini's shoulders while relieving her of her garments.

Please Tandy confide in me. Sister Tangela Mancini never heard her call her Tandy. They made love quietly and gently as changing a diaper on a baby's bottom.

Sister Tangela Mancini responded with feelings of pure longings and inquisitiveness of her own. In the darkness of the night she made it safely back to her quarters. The next morning Sister Tangela Mancini prayed long before anyone awaken for Morning Prayer. During Morning Prayer, she looked at the freshly varnished floor. Never again would she raise her eyelids. Eye contact wasn't worthy of her anymore. To her, she had committed her worst sin. After Morning Prayer, she went through her routine in a zombie state. She taught class in the morning and when lunch time came she ate alone trying to avoid Sister Bridget Johnson. Her afternoon duties were mainly paper work and typing the budget.

She paid the bills and interviewed all incoming possibilities. She answered the correspondence. Usually this was the part of the day that she enjoyed the most. This day, she didn't want to be involved in anything. She wanted to hide with her shame alone.

Sister Bridget Johnson entered the office, she was upon Sister Tangela Mancini before she realized her presence. Hello Sister, she boldly spoke. How is your day going? Sister Tangela Mancini's eyes never leaving her typewriter responded nervously. It's going very well.

Thank you Sister. I can't chat with you now these letters have to be typed and mailed by noon's end. I'm not here to chat with you Sister. Mother Mary sent me to tell you she needs you to lead the afternoon prayers. She has a migraine and asked me to deliver this message to you. Good day Sister. I hope your afternoon is as pleasant as your morning.

Sister Tangela Mancini opened up her orders from Mother Mary sent via Sister Bridget Johnson. They read. Tandy, Tandy, Tandy. You've sinned. To confess your sins to anyone else but God or higher uppers is a greater sin. You are not worthy of the vows you took when you gave yourself to God. I've got photographs to prove that fact.

If disbelief on your part enters your soul reach under your pillow for some truth. Once you find truth.

Use your accounting abilities to pay to the order of Bridget Johnson an Ethan Blackwell. In the amount of Ten thousand dollars, delivered at the exact place you found your truth within forty eight hours.

Sincerely the devil and Ms. Johnson.

P.S. In all sympathy, your sins demands destruction of this note. Sister Tangela Mancini scanned the ink on the duty roster wanting badly for it to fade, for her real duties to appear. She shook her head desperately trying to get a grip on herself. The typewriter in front of her started to get smaller as her surroundings darkened. She knew, she was on the verge of fainting.

She snatched the note from the envelope and stuffed it into her pocket. Seconds before tilting sideways.

She was awakened by one of her orphan sisters whose face would have made a heart patient check out. She had no blood circulation above her neck and her face was deathly pale from where Sister Tangela Mancini laid looking up. Please stay calm Sister, Mother Mary is on her way. Sister Tangela Mancini's head ached as her memory returned. As she remembered her ordeal she tried to straighten her disheveled disposition. Her body wouldn't cooperate. Mother Mary found her in that state. Mother Mary's maternal instincts for the girl reacted with disbelief. Sister Tangela Mancini insisted she was O.K., as Mother Mary walked her to her quarters speaking softly. What worries you my child? Is it anything that I shall seek the attention of a doctor? Oh no Mother I'm O.K., it's just fatigue. I probably been pushing myself too hard with the last group enrollment involving the handicap children. Mother I think I put overzealous feelings before my responsibilities that you've worked so hard to instill in me. Child don't bother yourself with what I've achieved, your health is our main concern.

Are you sure you are not in the need of a physician? No Mother I'm sure of it, thank you, I'll be fine.

Whatever it was, its pass, and if it flares again then I shall call you promptly. Thanks for your concern. Dear child I hate to leave you alone but my terrible headache is returning. I must go and see to it that our afternoon prayers are handled. Mother I'm sorry, I was not able to carry out your wishes with this afternoons prayers. Don't worry my child, I can always count on you to deliver Gods wishes some other time. Good night my child. I leave you in the hands of God now.

Sister Tangela Mancini disrobed, showered, and turned off all the lights and closed all the curtains. She laid on her bed in the darkness squinting her eyes making the dark get darker by holding her eyes closed then opening them.

She slept all afternoon and evening and through the night. She awakened at dawn one hour earlier before usual, showered again in the hottest water she could stand. She could not reach her filth and the hot water couldn't purify her mind. She made sure she was the last to arrive at Morning Prayer. She quietly sat in the first seat nearest the entrance. She prayed with her eyes closed tightly, rosary in hand. Am I worthy of prayer? Am I sane? I gave my life to you my Father. I've sacrificed my soul because that's what I believed I was put here for. Please Father help me now. She rose and hurried into the wash room and washed her hands up to her shoulders, watching the doorway through the mirror to make sure she was alone while she washed and prayed. The washing was a lesson Mother Mary taught her girls when they were very young. It wasn't mandatory teachings; a motherly lesson Mother Mary did on her own. They were taught to wash like she did now five times a day and some of the Sisters washed themselves all waking hours. Sister Tangela Mancini never understood why she washed so much until now as she scrubbed it all became clear. If she could not cleanse her soul, she would burn in hell for her sins. Sister Bridget Johnson entered the washroom. Good morning Sister. That soap only makes your soul like flames, fire in your hands, no need for soaping. Why did you not attend to your secretarial duties yesterday afternoon? Your gifted talents were needed, the bills have to be paid.

Did you not find truth under your mattress? Sister Tangela Mancini turned with a sharpness in her eyes that made Sister Bridget Johnson jump. Yes, yes, my good Sister your truth was indeed under my mattress but not the truth you believe. Your Ethan Blackwell played a dirty trick on us both Sister Tangela Mancini said gritting her teeth.

The so call truth he put under my mattress was pictures of you and him. In very compromising positions I should say. Sister Bridget Johnson went berserk as she reached for Sister Tangela Mancini in rage. You're a lie,

21

I shall beat the truth from you. The pictures were of you and I.

She attacked Sister Tangela Mancini so fast the soap dropped to the floor as Sister Tangela Mancini's hands went up to protect herself from the monster that emerged before her. In the struggle Sister Bridget Johnson's feet slipped on the bar of wet soap and she fell hitting her head on the concrete below making a blunt cracking sound that Sister Tangela would never forget.

Sister Bridget Johnson laid still as blood seeped from her wound and covered her face. Sister Tangela Mancini fled from the washroom pale and distraught.

Once in her quarters she shook thinking about what would happen once Sister Bridget Johnson's body was discovered. Then she would be exposed as the devil she knew she deserved this. She had to act fast. She hurried to the hall closet where the clean uniforms were kept for the kitchen crew. It was a good thing the workers wouldn't let Mother Mary control their lives. They long before demanded coveralls and white smocks be worn instead of the traditional. Sister Tangela Mancini changed in a hurry, yet dreading the awful decision that had to be made. She knew what was upon her knowing she could not escape penniless. She knew that in order to get money she had to commit yet another sin and that was to steal from the schools account. That meant changing again because she could not go to the office dressed in coveralls. She reversed again and returned to her holy garments. A total wreck is what she was as she was blinded by her tears. She made her way to the office nodding respectfully at those passing. She took a blank check from her desk and all the cash donations she could find. She returned to the closet to change back into the coveralls. They were a size to large but it didn't matter to her. All mattered now was her exit off the premises as quickly and quietly as possible leaving behind the only life she had ever known. There was only one place that she could go.

Somewhere in Texas. Torese Mehan wasn't sure where, either No Name or Georgetown. Mike Mehan and his wife Torese stopped to let their family relieve themselves. Torese ached for her home she shared with Mike.

They'd been on the road for a while now and they were finally returning home. They left their home three months ago from California heading east to Rhode Island where Mike's family lived. This had been the longest three months of Torese's life. She could have cared less about Mike's family, the shorter the stay the better and she never lied to him about how she felt. She only hoped their children wouldn't take after them.

They were rich, spoiled people and it was too late for her children because they already showed traits of being like Mike and his family. She hoped that they would take the genes of the family she had now and loved without a doubt. She'd been adopted since, shortly after her birth, and her parents wanted her something bad. She was the only child for four years until three homemade ones came along who was just as adored as she was.

Out loud to their friends while she was in the same room they got off their jollies. She became the talk of the crowd. She remembered her mother often saying many times that Reese was the prettiest she had. My other three are plain and homemade. She was prettier than her siblings and when she reached adulthood her skin toughened, her beauty shone through her eyes like rockets. In her mind her body wasn't her greatest asset her mind was. She'd been a straight A student since grade one. Her college professors encouraged her to walk in their shoes. Too bad she met and fell in love with Mike Mehan and married him. They had been together since eighth grade. He was the support and love that she always craved for. If only she had a family of her own in the beginning so she could make up for the family that she didn't have now. Wishful thinking on her part again. She always would think of Mike as an asshole.

Everyone returned from the rest rooms intact. One more hour of driving before Mike got them a suite, large enough to accommodate him, his wife, and the three little ones that he thought had attached themselves on him for a ride. He was used to spending money. They had three large rooms with adjoining doors with three queen size beds in each. A huge kitchen complete with a dishwasher an microwave. Everything but food. Their bathrooms came with smoke alarms and air purifiers. Their T.V, was equipped with HBO, while number one on their telephone put them in touch with the operator of their hotel.

Without a doubt Mike already had scoped the operator out long ago when they all entered the hotel. He now thought of her sweet body remembering her singing Hewey Lewis as Torese bedded down the twins in separate bedrooms. While their baby got to sleep alone as he did often. She joined Mike now after their children were sound asleep.

Walking into the living room area. Torese cuddled their baby. Why you bringing him in here honey? Oh I thought I'd let him fall asleep on me. He wasn't sleepy. He slept most of the day on the road. He'll probably fall asleep before either of us realizes it. If it's OK with you. Mike personality changed abruptly. He spoke low but firm. Please get your fucking brat the hell out of here Torese. This is my space now and I'm enjoying this room and it's late.

Torese turned and left the room knowing well that Mike was now agitated. She knew he was out of pot and had been for some time. And she knew her rich fucker couldn't afford to be without pot ever. Especially now that they were on the road with all his connections back where they lived.

Mike only brought along a half ounce of pot for the ride as he called it. He smoked it long before they reached their destination. When he reached his folks place it became a different story. In his folk's eyes and his siblings, he was a saint. His wife Torese was his problem and theirs.

She thought now, if only his family had gotten a whiff of the pot that he'd been smoking, they would finally know who was right and who the asshole was.

She also knew if they found out on this family trip east or got a whim that their son Mike had a pot problem. He would eventually beat the living shit out of his wife.

She produced three children for him and three grandchildren for his folks. She thought she had finally proven herself. Not likely...

Once she put her youngest to sleep. And finally heard Mike stop pacing. It was well after midnight. She sat alone at the kitchen table in their hotel glancing toward the living room where Mike was. Once in a while in her solitude she hoped that he would come out and keep her company. She hoped for conversation that he would never give her. The dripping faucet now drove her crazy. There was no stopping the drip. She got up twice to turn the nozzle to a different angle hoping to tame the drip. She couldn't shut it off. She wanted the whole sink out of the Hotel room. She ached for complete silence. She wanted to be alone with her thoughts. The drip wouldn't let her. Now come she thought, if she could rid herself of the twins by midnight. Get Mikes' pacing finally over with, and get the baby to go to sleep. How come now this drip now had to remind her of her loneliness. The drip hit the bottom of the sink with a rhythm. Sometime, it skipped a beat. Torese thought. If I can't control this drip. How am I expected to be able to control myself? She laughed at herself and took a swig of beer. Once upon a time, she loved her husband. Wanted him in every aspect. Mike Mehan could care less about her. He had his life and his money. His life was mainly his women and his work. He ate and slept every now and then. Now was his sleeping time. Torese dared not make any noise. She sat there and thought until she got a headache. She got into her pajamas and slid into the Hotel bed beside him. He didn't even know she was there. The baby cried promptly at seven. Torese pretended she didn't hear him hoping she was dreaming. Mike kicked her hard on her leg between her ankle and her knee. It hurt her bad and made her leg cramp as she jumped up and cared for her baby for his sake and her children's. When she reached the baby it was too late. The twins were awake. Hello Mommy. What's for breakfast? And good morning to both of you two honeys. Breakfast is not until I see clean faces and shiny teeth. Be quiet, dad is still sleeping so its shush time until he wakes, O.K.? The baby started to fuss. She catered to him quickly so Mike wouldn't wake up by his fussiness. The babies bottle was on the other side of the bedroom where Mike slept. Now she had to go through Mike to get her youngest his bottle.

Knowing his mood after he went to bed pot-less. She dreaded the move she had to make. She hushed the twins again giving them the baby. She entered the Master bedroom. Mike rolled from beneath the covers and glared at her. God damn you Reese, didn't you see I was sleeping. He scared her making her jump.

Didn't you see I was sleeping? Now get the hell in the other room with the kids. Didn't I get the suite large enough? Can you ever be satisfied? And for God's sake don't let those fucking kids make any more noise.

You, worthless piece of shit. Torese froze in her tracks. Baby Mitchell started to cry. Mike looked at her, I don't know why in the fuck I married your ass. A nanny could control our kids better than you. Torese made her way into the room without looking at him. She knew better. She also knew back talk would get her a black eye. Her lips were buttoned which still didn't help her out of this situation. Did you say go back to sleep. Who in the hell are you telling to go back to sleep? How in the fuck can I sleep with you going back and forth in here? You're dumber then I realize. Now get the fucking kids up and ready to go. I can't believe you can't control three fucking kids. Leave the fucking room and let me get dressed. Now he shouted loud enough to wake up the whole Hotel.

She hurried from the room closing the door behind her. Hushing the twins again. Dads's awake, we have to be quiet so we won't disturb him. She softly said starting to feed baby Mitchell his bottle that she retrieved anyway. Oh Mama for God's sake. Boy, did the twins sound just like their father. If Dad is awake Mama, then why do we have to be quiet? Can't we watch some cartoons? Please Maggie, not now. Just wait until Dad is fully awake. He's in a really sleepy mood. Michael the male twin spoke up. It's our choice Mom and you are out voted two to one. We're gonna go and ask him. Before the words left Michael's lips. Mike appeared in the doorway. He glared at Torese with hatred.

He glared at the kids and his eyes softened. Maggie, Michael get dressed and join Dad in the car. I'll take you to eat the best breakfast you ever had flashing his eyes at Torese he added, considering your Mothers cooking. You both got five minutes. If you're not in the car by then, I'm leaving both you guys. You Reese, you got two minutes. Both twins spoke at the same time. Mom where is our clothing?

Hurry Mom Michael blurted, let that brat feed by himself. Dad said to get us dressed right now.

Torese didn't know whether to shit or stay on the toilet. If she shitted now and took the bottle from baby Mitchells' mouth he would cry and make such a noise that Mike would take the twins to the car in their pajamas. He would leave her and the baby there just to prove a point. He often used her as a bad example to his children. They his audience she his example.

He was the holier than thou parent, as he showed that much in the delivery room insisting that the twins be named after both his parents. Margaret and Michael.

When he spoke to his twins about his wife, their Mother, he referred to her as their nanny. Four years later after baby Mitchell was conceived and born, Mike referred to him as the mail man's or the milk man's.

The more Mitchell took shape, Mike worsened. The baby's features were so much like his families, Mike rejected him more. Yet he insisted his name be Mitchell after his father's only brother. Still he wanted no part in dealing with the child. The twins were his pride and joy. He never had nothing to do with Mitchell nor would he even look at him. He loved his twins. The more he loved them the more they shone as his prefect Clones. They disrespected their Mom just as their Father did.

Mirrored Injustice

They did everything like he did, Maggie spoke up
first. Mom you're worthless. So much Mike's words.
Mom get us our clothes. If you don't right now Dad's
going to be mad. He's going to leave you and the brat.

Don't talk to her Maggie, Michael said, she's
useless. He walked into their room bringing their
suitcase to where Torese was. Pulling their clothes out to
find something suitable to wear as Torese swallowed
hard trying not to cry. Finally, in a hurry the twins
dressed themselves. Their clothing matched the
American flag. They wore stars with stripes, plaids with
sweats.

They ran from the Hotel room barefoot to the
parking garage where their Dad was once he finally
given up and left them all. Torese gathered up their
belongings as fast as she could holding on to crying baby
Mitchell as he dropped his bottle. She tripped running
after the twins out of breath with baby Mitchell swinging
from one hand and a half open suitcase dangling from
her other hand. Reaching the parking lot, she stumbled,
struggling to hold onto the baby. She dropped the
suitcase spilling its contents out on the ground. She
looked to see if Mike saw her clumsiness trying to gather
the belongings. Before she knew it he was upon her.
Snatching up the suitcase with one of his hands and
slapping her with his other.

You're a worthless piece of shit. Get your stupid ass in the car. Being led to the car didn't hurt her as much as being slapped. She was numb.

Nothing hurt her anymore, especially Mike's tactics. She vowed to herself before when she was pregnant after he punched her in her stomach which led her to have a so call nervous breakdown as he so delicately put it. That night she cried nonstop. The more she tried to control her tears her eyes produced more water. She cried for hours with every hour getting more out of control.

When she tried to stop crying her belly would flash before her, she'd cry harder. This cry was different. This time she knew she would never cry for him again.

Not in front of the children anyway, no matter how he mistreated her. He buckled baby Mitchell into his car seat, slammed the door hard enough to damage everybody's nervous system for life. He closed his driver side ever so gentle then buckled himself in. The twins looked on pouting.

Mama why'd you drop our clothes? They're all dirty now and we're not wearing them until you wash them, right Michael? Right Maggie. Torese didn't respond. Mike broke her thoughts by flinging his left hand at her making her flinch. He didn't hit her, just another way to demean her.

Mirrored Injustice

Instead he gave her a look that made her feel like a dirty wet rag. The best thing she could do now was nothing, what she always did. Any response from her and the three of them would be on her like flies on garbage. She stared outside trying to tell her mind to control her tears. Her body was his temple. Whenever the urge hit him, he would make love to her. That was his way of praying. He never went to church although his background was very religious. He pretended to his folks that he lived by their golden rule including church every Sunday. In reality he was a total asshole wipe out whose mere goals in his life were lying, beating and controlling his castle of puppets. He never ever laid a hand on his twins. Torese rode in silence. Her body still her mind in total turmoil. Thinking if I didn't think so much I wouldn't be here having nothing better to do but think. When Mike stopped to let the children pee, Torese cared for their baby. Not to the extent that she could recall things like how many times she changed him or when was his last bottle. They only occupied space with his rude disrespectful clone twins of him.

The twins treated Torese with as much respect as their father did. He said many time to them, she's not really your Mother, she is only our nanny, and I'm about to fire her because she is worthless. Mike pulled into a Hotel at the first sign of darkness. Tired Michael who had awaken from a deep sleep said daddy, if we sleep here I hope when me and Maggie wake up tomorrow you won't tell us not to watch cartoons. Michael you listen to me and only me. You know, you are the leaf of my family's tree. My oldest and only boy. He snickered. The baby is questionable. He shot Torese a cold blooded look saying you better not interrupt. I swear son it wasn't me who said you couldn't watch cartoons, it was your mother, excuse me, I mean nanny. Maggie piped up from a deep sleep. Yeah Michael that's just like her, she told us to be quiet this morning, 'cause you were sleeping. Dad tell her to be quiet for the rest of our trip like you said you would do before. Mike cleared his throat, Torese how come the twins couldn't watch cartoons this morning.

Torese didn't respond, her eyes didn't blink, her head never turned.

See guys, I told you she was stupid, Why don't we put her and her brat out after tonight, the next time we stop for a room we'll do it. You two have enough brains from my side of the family to learn to do without her not that she does all that much anyway. If you two had her families brains no telling where you would be, who knows, where she comes from anyway, remember my precious portentous college professors, she was adopted and what does that mean? No life, no background. She doesn't even know who she is. Whoever says, we drop her and the brat off, raise their hands.

Mirrored Injustice

Both Michael and Maggie's hands flew up as fast as it took Torese to turn her head around. Her response was only because she thought, she was as stupid as they said she was. She knew their hands would raise but she hoped maybe somehow they would tell their Father to fuck off. And say Mama is an alright person. Not today, tonight, or ever would she hear those words. They both were still too young. Mike parked and ushered the twins toward the Hotel, only to find a no vacancy sign blinking away. It's all your fucking fault Reese. If you didn't have to stop all the fucking time to feed that fucking brat, we would have been here earlier before the rooms were all booked up. Now what the fuck are we supposed to do?

Mike honey, Torese spoke softly trying to touch his arm. We could try another Hotel that one across the highway looks open. Shut the fuck up. Let's go, goddam it. I'll drive all fucking night if I have to, maybe I'll get lucky and have an accident. I'll do anything so I won't have to look at your fucking face anymore.

It was two more days of abuse for Torese and baby Mitchell, before they reached Laguna Beach California. As they pulled up in front of their home, Torese quietly asked. "Honey wouldn't it be easier to park in the garage, so we can unload". Shut the fuck up slut. You just tell me where the keys are to my fucking car. They'd driven Torese's station wagon for the trip. She whimpered, "There inside the house in the first cupboard on the right, in the kitchen, on the top shelf.

Mike raised the garage door with the remote standing outside of the car parked in front of their front door pointing it in that direction. He then, entered the house, and retrieved his car keys. Taking the keys from the station wagon with him. With the house keys attached to them.

Torese gathered up the children out of the station wagon and headed for the front door. As they approached the front door, Mike's Porsche screeched backing out. He stopped long enough to close the garage with his window rolled down using the remote control.

He drove away.

Thanks a lot Mike, Torese said out loud. At lease you could have opened the front door for us. She gave Maggie the baby and went back to the station wagon to get the keys from the ignition, as they were now standing at the front door for him to open it. Damn him that bastard took the keys. How are we supposed to get inside? She reached for the remote control to open up the garage door. It was gone too. She became pissed. Mama, Maggie yelled, this baby is getting heavy. Come on, I have to go pee. Torese wiped her forehead trying to think of what to do next. Daddy took the keys honey, we're locked out. Maggie started to cry. I'm going to pee on myself you dummy, open the door now!

Mirrored Injustice

Torese finally couldn't handle anymore tension. She took off her sweater and wrapped it around her fist. She broke the living room window, closest to the lock. She cleared the remaining glass from around the window panes. Then lifted her biggest child Michael inside to do the deed. He opened the front door as piss ran down Maggie's legs.

Maggie go clean yourself up, her mother said putting baby Mitchell down in his day bed in their living room. Michael you come help me with the luggage.

Michael and Maggie obeyed their mother perfectly well when their dad wasn't around. It took Torese hours to unpack and put away their things enough so the house was livable. After she fed them all, the baby fell asleep. The twins too, in front of the T.V. Torese mixed herself her first martini. She didn't expect Mike for hours which she hoped would turn into days. She'd put up with his abuse for years. Now after this particular event, the here and now, especially after the trip facing and dealing with his family. She realized what a complete phony he was with his fake life. Somehow this moment was sour. She wasn't sure anymore if she'd ever loved him. She wasn't sure if she knew how to love any human being. She never had a best friend besides Mike in the beginning. That was like ages ago. The last good years in her life. There weren't many people in her life.

Her teen years were nice. High school got mixed up in her mind with now, most of the time.

Before their vacation. Torese had only the best to be thankful for.

Which included Mike. His salary over exceeded them for the time he put in. Tennis and Golf, was what they paid him for. She usually drove his Porsche. And his friend's thought of her as his wife.

A man's lady with a life time membership to their socialite club Mike belonged to their private little section of Laguna Beach.

Torese was gorgeous, but she dressed herself down. All his friends accepted her but only for her abilities to birth Mikes' children and be his wife. According to his friends philosophy, everything was Mike's. His wife, their children, and their friends.

She was his shadow always in the background. He boasted about her as she played her beauty down again and again. She'd often think to herself how she wouldn't become one of Mike's toys. This vacation was a shit or get of the pot kind of situation. She was on her second Martini hoping that he was happy where he was.

Noise startled her as Mike stormed into their home which overlooked Hillcrest Drive North of Laguna Beach. Their home was immaculate as were all the others around them. At night, if all neighbors kept their kitchen lights on once the sun went down the glow overcame the ocean waters. The scene became a picture worth painting by a thousand painters. Tonight, Torese wasn't in the mood. She had shitted and now if only she could leave the pot boiling. She waited for him to enter their bedroom. She took one look at him and decided it wasn't worth her time to deal with the asshole. She took the only thing she had. A phone number her Mother had given her a long time ago. As her Mother gave it to her she said, if you're ever desperate, call this number she remembered her Mother saying about every Christmas as she spoke to her about her adoption. Torese put the phone number in her pocket now as she walked out the door away from Laguna Beach.

It started to rain. The water felt good to her. Torese apparently hadn't been alone for a long time. Loneliness was a strange feeling. She could deal with the strangeness because of the piece of paper she had tucked in her pocket. She looked at it protecting it from the water that drenched her. She remembered the conversation her mother had with her, discussing that very piece of paper. As her Mother put it in her hand: Honey you are my child truly. I love you. With all my love I deliver this message with ease. Here is an address that belongs to a very good friend of mind. She was there through thick and thin. She was there, when you were born. She asked me to tell you if there was ever a time you needed her or someone besides myself. For you to call on her. Honey you know she sent you many gifts every birthday and Christmas. All the gifts came for your entire life. I lied and told you all the gifts were from Dad and I.

The reason I lied is not important now. Please don't judge me or your father until you've heard from this friend, if you ever will. I've completed my task. It's up to you now to understand.

I just ask you to remember that I love you and I'll always will no matter what happens in your life or-mine. Now in the rain Torese was on her way to find the person that cared so much about her. She was wet, cold; coughing and scared. She hurt for her children. Mike never entered her mind. She tripped and fell in the mud. Passed out in the lonely, wet, deserted night.

Tacy Peruvian lived alone most of her life. She wanted it that way. At the age of fifty, she still maintained her girlish looks given to her at birth. She never married and had no family. She once had a sister that died young, which was a long time ago, in her other life. This was her new life. It been this way ever since, she lost her only sister more then twenty years ago. Her sister was four years younger. She died a horrible death. Tacy didn't deal with that life anymore. Her downfall in her other life gave her the strength for this new life. She always believed in the unknown. Telling a persons whole card was only reaping what they only knew of.

Mirrored Injustice

Now she was a Gypsy living on the white oceans of
Kaho'olawe Hawaii. Established to friends as Tacy the
friend no one should be without. To vacationers she was
the greatest fortune teller that ever lived. She never
minced words. Her money was a safe alternative to her
life. Happiness was the having achieved set goals. Inner
peace and self-worthiness was the fortune she put men,
money, happiness all in one tongue.

She never succeeded in either. She had a calmness
about her that made everyone who came in contact with
her love her. She was secure in her life. Her
surroundings were small but quaint. Her heart large, but
naive. She received a phone call from a friend's
daughter. A niece of hers but maybe not really a niece.
She hardly tried to remember anymore. She knew the
girls voice and she knew her parents were vacationing in
the South of France. The girls parents confided in Tacy
every chance they got. The Operator repeated herself.
While Tacy gathered her thoughts. I have a person to
person collect call from Tia Morgan for Tacy Peruvian.
Tia spoke up loud. May I speak to her please? Hello, this
is Tacy Peruvian. Will you accept the call? Yes. Ms.
Tacy Hi, this is Tia Morgan. She started to cry. Honey
calm down. What is it? Tia was frantic. I hope you
know me. I'm in trouble. I have nowhere else to go. I've
never met you. You've sent me lots of gifts. My parents
talked about you all the time.

Excuse me if I'm babbling.

No child, go on, I'm listening. Do your parents know you're phoning me? No they are on vacation. I'm flying to Kaho'olawe. I have no choice, please don't turn me away. All I have is your phone number. The operator told me this phone call is to Kaho'olawe, I need your address that's if...

Tia paused. If I'm welcome. You are welcome here, Tia anytime that's if. Shouldn't you call your parents first and inform them that you're coming here? Tia started to cry hard out of control. I need you. You promised me with the notes and all the gifts, she sniffed. Waiting for her fairy God Mother to speak. Silence passed and Tia broke down. Listen Ms. Tacy. You made my parents a promise and I'm on my way. She hung up.

Tacy ignored the tantrums from the girl believing her parents would call her in the morning. Ten minutes later the phone rang again. Tacy was tired. She opened up her fortune telling booth promptly at Six A.M., four hours away from the ringing telephone.

She lifted the phone from its hook. Hello is this Ms. Tacy Puruvian? Yes, this is, who is this? My name is Tangela Mancini. I was given your phone number from Mother Mary. A very good friend of yours from Philadelphia. Tacy instantly became alert. Who is this? At first she thought it was a joke. The voice kept talking. It's me Ms. Tacy. Remember the kid you've been sending presents to? And all the notes, all my life. Telling Mother Mary, I'm a special person. The kid you been sending presents to. Remember me? Please think I'm special now. Who is this Tacy yelled?

This is Tangela. Sister Tangela Mancini sobbed so hard her words slurred.

I've left the convent. I'm on my way seeking you. I have little choice. You are the only one I know of outside of this church. You made a lot of promises and all to me. I need to talk to you about something. Therefore, I shall be there as soon as I can catch a flight. Good night Ms. Tacy.

We shall meet soon.

Tacy sat straight up in her bed now. The fortunes and the dope fiends she put up with everyday couldn't compare to what she had just heard.

Her blood pressure rose. She was shocked. The phone rang again. Ms. Tacy Peruvian please. This is Tacy she said trying to put her eye balls back into their sockets. Who is this?

This is the Los Angeles hospital calling on the behalf of Torese Mehan. All Hell broke loose. Tacy never lost control before now she frantically reached for her anxiety medications.

Is this some kind of fucking joke? Don't fuck with me anymore tonight. She slammed the phone down. The operator rang the phone again. Don't hang up Ms.

this is the Los Angeles County hospital calling. There is
a person here tonight unconscious. The only phone
number we found on her was this number. Do you have
a clue to who she is? Her name is Torese Mehan. Tacy
Peruvian fainted. She slept for the night with the phone
off the hook. She regretted ever closing her eyes in the
beginning or opening them now. She feared for what
today would bring.

Tacy awakened half on the bed and half off. For the
first time her persona was in disarray. She didn't wash
her face or brush her teeth.

She was dazed. She took another Darvocet and
thought fuck it. This headache is only because of the bad
dreams I had last night. I really should send more gifts
to the girls.

Her doorbell rang. She slipped her slippers on and
headed for the door. Forgetting the dream, she had last
night. She opened the door. The person that she saw
was the prettiest human being she had seen in a long
time. With the Darvocet kicking in she didn't recognize
who the person was. Whoever you're looking for honey,
I'm sorry. You've got the wrong house. She slammed the
door turning toward the staircase. The bell rang again.
She turned and flung open the door. She knew that she
had lost as her tears rolled down her face. Please Ms.
Tacy. I've come a long way. I'm Tia, your Goddaughter.
I need to talk to you. I'm the one who called you last

night. May I come in? Tacy could barely focus. Damn she said to herself. Here comes that damn dream again. She rubbed her temples. Hi, Yes, I remember now. You are Tia aren't you? Yes, and you must be Ms. Tacy. Yes, that's me come inside. Do your parents know where you are? No ma'am, I'm all alone. I really have a big headache Tacy said, I thought I dreamed you last night. Before Tia could respond the bell rang. Excuse me, I'll get rid of whoever it is, then I'll see you to the airport. Tacy walked to the door. The sight before her made her head hurt more, the room spun. She turned to Tia. Girl go upstairs now! Tia ran relieved heading for the nearest bed she could find. Tacy stared at the second most beautiful person exactly like the one who exited two seconds before. She was stunned again as she faced the girl. Rubbing her temples again and speaking slowly. May I be of some assistance to you? Hello Ms. Tacy. My name is Sister Tangela Mancini. May I please come into your home? Tacy stepped back unbelieving. Please come inside, who did you say you were? I'm Sister Tangela Mancini. The Mother Superior and this piece of paper tells me you are my only confidant.

Please am I welcome? Tacy's vision blurred. Excuse me honey, I'll be right back. She went into her nearest bathroom and gulped two Tylenol down. The Sister sat politely on the love seat not to disturb her surroundings waiting in her shame. Tacy returned from the bathroom.

Honey you must have come a long way. I welcome your visit. Tacy thought hard seeking the right words. What about the convent? To my understanding, I thought you were happy. The doorbell rang again. Excuse me Tangela honey, I'll answer the door while you rest up a bit. Go upstairs into the first door on your left, there's an adjoining door that leads to a bathroom where you can freshen up. You will be comfortable there until we can talk further. The tired Sister didn't respond. Rest was the best thing that she could think of at this point. Tacy pointed her in the direction of the stairs. Tangela disappeared up the steps finding the first door on the left. Tacy headed toward the ringing door figuring whoever was ringing her doorbell deserved a good cussing out. The person lay on the bell. Tacy swung open the door using profanity to show that she was not to be fucked with. Just who in the fuck do you think you are ringing my fucking bell like that? She began to cry as she focused on the figure. Hi the figure said. Are you my sweet Tacy Peruvian. I'm sorry to disturb you. I'm Torese Mehan. She were a perfect clone to the other two species held up in Tacy's two guest bedrooms upstairs resting. Tacy had no argument for this girl. Please come inside precious. Yes, you have the right address indeed. Tacy embraced the girl. Don't say anything, I know you're tired. Tacy dried her eyes with the back of her hand. She was at her most exposed point in her life. She led Torese to the same room that Tangela and Tia shared with her only minutes earlier. Torese, Tacy hoarsely spoke, or do you go by Reese. Yes, Reese is fine. O.K., then listen Reese, I've had a rough day today. Would it be O.K., if we continued this conversation later this afternoon. Sure but I'm not sure how to address you. I'm not sure who exactly you are to me. Just call me Aunt Tacy. That will do for now. Tacy led Torese to the guest bedroom on the first floor and showed her the adjoining bathroom.

Tacy locked the front door knowing she wouldn't have to answer it anymore today. The clones were all here now. Now she had to prepare for the showdown, she could no longer prevent.

As tired as they all were they all slept through the evening and straight through the night. Tacy awaken at four a.m., showered quietly not to disturb her house guests. Chuckling to herself, she decided to call them her personal clones. Calling them clones took less time than to think of them as individuals.

The showdown would take place in Tacy's fortune telling quarters. Her fortune telling quarters was a bricked Tepee structure at the side of the house, but had one entrance that connected to a house from the back it was a mirrored room with three individual small dressing rooms all mirrored. Another entrance on the side was off the curb and open for the public to enjoy serenity if they choose. It had an inviting settee and never closed to public. Yes, yes, she shook her head. That's where it should be. She pondered about her outfit, then selected it carefully. Her outfit played a big part in the way she decided to handle the situation. It took hours before her appearance was completed. It was now almost seven a.m. Still not being able to put names with faces yet. She entered the nearest bedroom to hers and the nearest Clone.

Honey wake up. Tangela sat up still half asleep. Get up honey and put your clothes back on. Its seven o'clock. Meet me down stairs. Go outside of the front door and to the corner at the end of the house, turn to your left. The door you see is the door to my shop. It will be open. Go in. Don't ask any questions. I know this sounds weird but I need you to wait in one of the booths with the curtains pulled shut. Don't open them until I come for you. I will explain everything to you when we meet and then, you will know who I am to you. You have fifteen minutes. Be there at seven fifteen. I need your word that you'll do exactly as I say even if you have to wait for me for forty-five minutes. It's very important, do you understand? Yes, I'll be there Tangela said used to obeying orders. Thanks Tacy said I hope I can count on you. The booth you are to wait in is number one. Tacy left her to dress. Tacy gave the same speech to her other two clones with different times.

Mirrored Injustice

Seven thirty to the second Clone and seven forty-five, she told the third Clone. Giving them each different booth numbers. All three must wait for her in closed booths. She walked back to her bedroom and paced until eight a.m. After she was sure the stage was set, she watched nonchalantly from her bedroom window as each girl entered the shop. Tacy dreaded what was ahead of her. She put out her cigarette in the overflowing ash tray that accumulated during the three hours it took her to dress. She headed down the steps and out the front door. Half glancing at the neon sign blinking. It blinked. Let Tacy read you.

She entered the door beneath the sign and closed all the blinds then drew all the curtains. Making the shop absent of daylight. She plugged in her special lights that were designed to enhance the personalities of her patrons by blinking blue, green, orange and red colors one after another. The colors changed everything in the room to the color it shone for thirty seconds or more.

The colors then bounced off the mirrors coloring every square inch of the room.

Tacy sat at her desk that held her crystal ball along with all her other psychic paraphernalia that took to preform her job. She called Tia, Tangela, Torese. Please come out now. All three girls nervous as cats about the weird situation pushed their mirrored doors open. Each abiding by Tacy's rules entered the mirrored room. The scene was perfect. Tacy's psychic personality was everywhere. Mirrors engulfed the three clones as the lights colored them. They each thought they was trapped in a circle of reflections. Then, realizing in the mirrors that all the images were the same. The same faces, same bodies. Different clothing. Impossible.

The two men in the suits that glimpsed Tia at the airport were totally pissed at the exact time the Clones were turning in their own reflections. The two men also were ransacking Tia's parents' condo in Aspen. No nick knack was left untouched. They tore the place apart. Minutes later they came across Tia's diary. The last entry was two days ago. It stated how she made love to the Cobra and that was the last time she saw him.

The last thing the suited men wanted to know about was Tia's sex life. Their names were Kent Dodge and Mickey Clemones. They were from New York. Kent Dodge threw the diary against the wall. Mickey talk to me, there is nothing in this piece of shit that tells us anything. O.K., Kent man don't get so hyper, calm your ass down, Don't tell me to calm down man, that bitch got what we need and we don't know where the fuck she is. She must have heard every fucking thing we said. I say we go finish Ryckman off now. Man calm yourself, Mickey said, You're not thinking clearly. If he's not already dead? Then he must be in the hands of the authorities by now. Well we gotta do something besides sit here and listen to your dumbass make excuses. Kent was delirious with anger. I'm scared Mick, what the fuck do we do now, come on communicate with me man, never mind. You mother fucking wuss, your extra change weighing my pockets down. I'll do the job myself, you're dead meat.

Kent shot Mickey faster than it took to glance at the clock on the wall to tell the time. Mickey shook a little then took his proper place in the world beyond. He laid in shambles. Violence was far and in between. Far being about every fifteen years if that in Aspen Colorado.

The sheriffs were not lazy but settled. They felt their balls every time they arrested someone for driving under the influence. They often ran and slammed into each other's vehicles in the pursuit of a chase. Now the officers had a serious crime.

It was their first crime since one rich lunatic shot another rich lunatic. Countless times from behind a rock. The next day's daily rag printed everything they thought to be true. In our sacred safe town, a man was found dead in a local Condo. The family that lived in the Condo was away when the death occurred. What the daily rag didn't know was that Tia did not go with her parents to France.

Kent Dodge flew to New York alone, fuming having to explain the death of his comrade. Tony Ryckman being dead or not being dead. The missing five million dollars lost in the briefcase. It became the death of him. Kent Dodge disappeared off the face of the earth without an outline of a body or an explanation to his family. If he had any.

The man behind the desk giving the orders demanded silence. He stared intensely at his men around him. His bald head nodded up an down, while he clamped his jaws tight. His face contracted inwards showing his veins protruding from the insides of his tight round self.

Gentleman to solve a problem one must eliminate the source. Our main concern is the briefcase. I don't see a reason to mince words or people. The first one of you who finds the briefcase gets one half of its contents. This meeting is adjourned. He stood tall. All his men surrounded him protecting him without so much as a nod. Once everyone exited he waved his bodyguards away. Then Quintin Lovost laid his sorry bald head on his desk.

In his otter office his men sipped their last bits of cold coffee turning their Styrofoam cups up to their heads then throwing them everywhere but in the trash cans. They gave excuses talking over one another excusing themselves. All Quintin's men left the building besides his main bodyguards and Norway. Norway was out to prove a point or die trying. If he couldn't prove this point, then this was the beginning of his sacrifice.

Mirrored Injustice

He exited with the others but turned the corner to the men's bathroom. He relieved himself knowing the others should have been out of the building by now. He backtracked into Quintin's private office this time no invitation was needed.

Norway was to die for his cause. He gave Quintin's bodyguards a line about how he left his briefcase in the office and how Quintin was adamant so much now about briefcases. One bodyguard opened the door with a key for him talked with Quintin for a second, then gave Norway the go ahead to enter the office.

He found Quintin trying to rest again putting his head back down on his desk allowing the asshole to come back in and retrieve his briefcase.

Lift your head up mother fucker and don't say a word.

Norway motioned Quintin around in his swivel chair with his finger while he had his Ruger pointer at him. Don't reach for anything you Slime ball. Don't buzz for your pussies either. Do as I say and we both live. Push the intercom slowly or you die. Tell all your guards to go to lunch. It's your choice, make one crazy move and I kill you first and then your assholes may or may not kill me, you won't live to know. I'm ready to die, are you? Quintin did as Norway told him, not because he was afraid, but because his age had finally caught up with him. Now he sort of took pride in this young asshole having the guts to fuck with him. Reminded him of himself in his younger days. He pressed the intercom silently laughing to himself. Seeing how far this crazy young man would go. Fellows I have a lady coming up in ten minutes from fifty second street. You all know Norway don't you? Well we don't want to scare the lady do we. You all go to lunch. Plain English y'all get your asses the fuck out of my building. Now!

Quintin lived his life up to now with protection from this kind of thing. He dealt with people like Norway before and he knew, he would have the fucker dead and buried before long. Now all his men were getting lost on his orders. He pushed his chair outward enough to reach his revolver from his desk drawer. I said mother fucker don't try anything. Quintin straightened up now not sure about the move, he made relieving his body guards. Norway pushed him out of his chair on the floor and put the gun to his head. Tell me where the fucking papers are now and I'll let you live. You sent a friend of mine on a wild goose chase and now I'm gonna count to three. One, two three. Tell me shitface your time is up. He cocked the trigger. Speak now or forever hold your fucking peace. He put the nozzle of his gun in Quintin's mouth.

Quintin started to cough and choke. Norway pulled his gun back to hear him. The information you want is in the right hand bottom drawer. The key is in my wallet. Don't shoot me. It better be you slez ass or I'll kill you for sure. Norway retrieved the key from Quintin's pocket and opened the drawer never taking his eyes off Quintin. He opened the drawer with the key and there was a safe with a combination lock. Don't play games with me mother fucker. Tell me the fucking combination now! Quintin said the numbers slowly. Norway opened the safe that was made to look like an ordinary drawer.

Taking his eyes off Quintin for a split second to glance over the papers. He bought his eyes from the paper to Quintin nodding in agreement when he saw the boss man aiming a gun at his head.

He hit Quintin fast in the top of his bald head with the butt of his revolver, knocking the gun from his hands. Then he hit him again for safe keeping. Norway stashed the folder under his coat. The highest paid associate in the world he considered himself. Getting the briefcase was only his beginning. After he accomplished that task. His next move would be to take Quintin for everything for what he was worth. Norway caught the next plane out heading for Kaho'olawe Hawaii.

At the convent in Philadelphia Pennsylvania Mother Mary slept peacefully. Sister Eliza Adams awaken her from her sleep. Mother,

Mother, please wake up. There's been a terrible tragedy in our washroom. Sister Adams didn't give Mother Mary time to respond. The holy superior had no time to cover herself as the young Sister yanked her up into a sitting position ranting hysterically. Mother sit up Sister Eliza Adams belted. Mother Mary could hardly focus on the young girl. It was late into the night beyond the hours of the A.M. I said Mother wake the fuck up Sister Eliza Adams yelled. Then she automatically began praying for the almighty to forgive her for using the devil's words. Mother Mary had not taken her vows that long ago for her to lose her composure now. She looked at her beloved daughter child. Sister Aliza Adams, I think you are out of control.

I'm sorry Mother please come with me. I hope you are awake and I beg your forgiveness for using the devil's words to get your attention. Mother listened quietly. There is a dead body in our wash room. Mother Mary rushed from her bed grabbing her robe on her way out, following Sister Eliza Adams to wherever she was being led. They entered the washroom with Mother Mary half expecting to find a dead animal that wandered in from the cold. Mother Mary froze in her tracks standing staring at Sister Bridgett Johnson's body. She bent over her daughter-child searching for a pulse feeling under her neck for some Kind of livelihood. Nothing.

Mother Mary then waved the crying Sister to silence giving the dead nun her last rites.

Mirrored Injustice

Cover the body Sister, I need to make a phone call.
Sister Eliza ran screaming from the wash room asking
her almighty God to forgive her for her cowardly ways.
Mother Mary covered the body with a wall hanging that
was hand knitted by one of her most talented girls.
Ironically it was a picture of Jesus nailed to the cross.
Mother Mary dialed father Jessup's number.

The phone rang to what seemed like an eternity to
Mother Mary.

Forgive me Father for disturbing you at this hour.
This is me, Mother Mary. There has been trouble here
and I need your assistance. Father George Jessup was
the head monk at the Monastery located three miles
away on Eighty second and Lands down Ave. The
oldest building left intact enough to renovate after the
area overdeveloped becoming a major highway and
shopping district. Many of the old buildings near the
Monastery had long ago been turned into something
else. Father Jessup's eyes twinkled at the sound of
Mother Mary's voice. I'm awake, what seems to be the
trouble? Father can you come to the convent at once?
It's a matter that cannot be discussed over the phone. Ok
I'm on my way. I should be there in twenty minutes.
Thank you Father, I'll be waiting. Mother Mary then
knelt and prayed waiting in anticipation for Father
Jessup's arrival. Seeing his headlights park in the
distance didn't break her thoughts. She met him at the

door. Father Jcssup welcome, thanks for coming considering these circumstances. Please come inside. Let me help you with your coat and hat. Follow me. He followed her into the study and she closed the door behind them. I've got a problem George. One of my girls met with ill fate. Mary in all the years I've known you, I can't think of a problem with your girls that you ever needed my assistance to handle.

Follow me. She led him up the spiral staircase then through the hall on the second floor. Facing him directly she 'looked as if she wanted to say something then thought against it. As they reached the wash room in silence Mother Mary turned to look at him again before pushing the door open. I'm afraid George that Sister Bridgett Johnson is dead. He stood over the body pulling the handmade blanket from the dead Sisters face.

Does anyone else know about this? Yes, I'm afraid so. Sister Eliza Mans found her, then she called on me for my expertise. I calmed her down enough and made her promise to remain silent at least for now until I can take care of things quietly. It looks to me to be some sort of accident, there's water on the floor, an look at that soap over there against the wall, maybe she slipped. Father wouldn't she have had to slip a might hard to meet this fate? No not if she hit her head on the basin before she hit the floor. Father there's something else I failed to mention. I hope it's not another body Mary. No

not another body, thank God. But it's still a problem.
Sister Tangela Mancini has disappeared.

Baby Mitchell's cries woke up his dad. Mike buried
his face by putting the pillows on top of his head. But
just until Reese would calm the noise. She didn't, baby
Mitchell continued to scream turning his screams into
choking sounds.

Mike started to count. He was hung over to the
max. Slipping into the house in that condition was no-
big deal, but Reese letting that brat cry was. He jumped
up throwing the pillows and covers off him. He
slammed open the adjoining doors hard. Reese control
the fucking brat or I'll kick your fucking ass. His yelling
woke the twins from a quiet sleep.

Mom, Michael yelled grouchy from his sleep. Mom,
mom, I know you hear that damn baby crying. Why
don't you shut him up! Twin number two Maggie came
to life. Hush Michel, I'll handle this. I'll make her quiet
that brat. Dad you be quiet too. She jumped out of her
bed pouncing into baby Mitchell's room knowing that's
where she would find her dumb Mother, she then
decided that after discovering the crying baby was alone
that Mom was probably downstairs cooking breakfast
without her brat. Maggie made a sharp turn and skipped
down the stairs into the kitchen knowing she would
corner and curse her opponent. Mike's head pounded.

He was making sounds that he usually made when he was unattainable to any indulging species.

Maggie entered his room. Dad, Mom's not in the kitchen, is she in here? No she isn't butt brain, go back where you came from and find her. Tell her to get her ass in here right now. Roar. Roar, was a game Mike played with his children since they occupied his space. At play time when they were little he'd act like a lion and tickle their stomachs until they did what he said, then he would say Roar. and they would go laughing all the way. This time Roar meant to do what he said now! Baby Mitchell cried on. Damn it, did y'all find that fucking bitch yet? The twins searched for Torese throughout the house. Mom, Mom they yelled. Mike snatched the screaming baby from his crib stomping off to join in the search for his wife. He wanted so bad to slap the God forsaken shit out of her. He stumbled over some suitcases. That stupid bitch didn't even put away the fucking luggage. Wait till I find her. He met the twins on the landing of the stairs. Did y'all find her? They looked dumbfounded and puzzled. No we didn't Dad, she's not here. Oh yes she is he said heading for the laundry room. He ran straight into the pool table in the den before reaching the laundry room smashing his upper leg bringing pain into his already aching hung over body. Where the fuck are you Reese?

Mirrored Injustice

Thank God he started to limp because if he had of found her now it would have been total devastation because then he tripped over the ottoman banging his brains out.

Shit, ouch, what the fuck is going on in this fucking house. He still held on to baby Mitchell. He was in a rage and out of breath. When I lay my hands on you, I'll find your ass. He took one room at a timer, over and over again while his twins watched.

Their silent already knowing stare enraged Mike more. Go to your room he yelled at them after not being able to find Torese. Here, take this baby with you. They knew he was starting to lose control. He threw the baby at them and Maggie caught him. He went back up to his bedroom to wait for Torese.

Tacy's fortune teller shop connected to the side of her home. The thoughts going through the minds of her Clones were, what Tacy denied herself of for too many years. Out of the darkness she spoke. The neon lights focused on her attire. The darkness blinking her face absent. Her throat dried up making her voice masculine. The chill she felt made her sneeze. Huh chew. Excuse me. Ladies please meet each other for the first time. She dabbed her hanky to her nose. According to the minutes between you three ladies, you are Tia, Tangela and Torese. Individuals indeed. Two minutes apart each. Planted from the same delicate seed.

Neither Clone spoke. Their heartbeats were too loud anyway to hear voices from each other. They stared at one another intensely. Their hearts beating faster beat by beat. Blood fear raced through their beings. They burst all at once screaming, What is this? What's going on? Who are these others? Who are you people? Colors blinked in their faces. They cried at each other. Tacy emerged from the darkness, holding out her arms, extending more than comfort, real closeness which neither girl had never known before and didn't know they missed. Come to me ladies, lean on your Aunt Tacy now.

Like programmed robots they each obeyed. They all embraced Tacy crying twenty-five years of tears. Cry hard, cry hard, Tacy squeezed them tightly. She planned this scene many years ago, now the tears running down her face was not included in her original plans. This moment was worth all the feelings she suppressed all these years.

She never regretted anything she did in her life up until this point. All she'd gained this far, this scene was a step back in memories deeper then she cared to remember. Her clones had finally come to her. She cried and hugged them with all her might. Girls ssh, I need to explain some things. Tacy broke the embrace reaching to shut off the blinking neon lights. She opened the blinds letting light into the parlor.

Mirrored Injustice

The daylight blinded the clones. They covered their faces. They were so much alike it hurt Tacy's eyes.

Ladies I must talk now, let's go back to the house. Follow me, I'll Ring a service for some breakfast.

Tacy led and they followed in fantasy waiting to awaken from their spells. Tacy was sorry that the situation wasn't handled more as planned. They all walked out and entered the main entrance get comfortable ladies. Neither clone responded as their tears poured from their eyes.

Not one of them had experienced anything of this nature before.

This is as hard for me girls as it for each of you three. I don't really know where to begin. I need all of your help now. We have the rest of our lives for tears. I must explain to each of you what you need to know to unravel this mystery. Let's see. I'm at a loss for words. Here girls take some tissues. Each of you blow hard. I'm a fortune teller. My name is Tacy Peruvian. My profession doesn't allow me to be at a loss for words. Tia Cut her off. Ms. Tacy she dug out the words.

These two people here must be my sisters or siblings, look at us we look alike but I'm not adopted how can this be? It's not possible.

Honey if you let me finish, I'll tell you how it is possible.

No bitch you let me finish. Who are you and who am I? Please don't answer me. How can I forget you're at a loss for words, aren't you?

Well lady let me tell you one fucking thing I'm lost too. I'm lost for every fucking thing that I ever believed in, all my life. Got it? Excuse me, may I say something? Another clone spoke. I'm Tangela Mancini.

Sister Tangela Mancini. I don't know where and how I've become. I was orphaned young. Still I fail to understand what's taking place now.

Never mind. Never mind my ass Torese spoke. I just left the only reason I ever existed, my kids. Never mind ain't to be dealt with now my Sister. Wait a minute Tacy yelled over the clones. You three seem to think I'm utterly fucking crazy. Impossible. Take a look around yourselves. Look at each other, accept what you see then maybe we can talk like rational people.

Yeah right lady, I don't know how you did this or who the fuck these two people are you paid to look like me. Lots of surgery huh! You want my folks money don't you? Should I try to escape now or should I wait for you three to kill me? I know y'all all is in this together. Tia's voice rose. It was her loudest voice she could muster up before her throat started to ache. No honey, this is for real. Wait, I have something that I'll solve all your suspicions, I'll be right back.

Tacy left and returned. Here ladies she said handing out an object. Take a good look. Torese snatched the object from her hands. It was a gold Locket. That's mine, I must have dropped it.

Oh no its mine Tia grabbed it from Torese's hand. Tangela reached for it saying something as Tacy relieved it from all three Clones. Excuse me I'll take it. We each have one. The only four like this one in the world. I know neither of you would leave home without it so check yourselves please.

All our names are engraved on it. All our names start with the letter 'T' don't it. Not a coincidence. Mines is the only one here that has a picture of all four of us together in it. May I see it? Sister Tangela whispered. Tacy gave her locket to Tangela. She took the locket holding it tender, opening it seeing the photo of them for the first time in her life as kids. No mistaking any of them to be who they were, she passed it to Tia. I accept the truth in my eyes now and I pass this locket along hoping you each will find the truth also. Then we can sit together and sort this all out. If you all will allow me

I will say a prayer of thanks. Maybe I've finally found my heritage. No, Tia cried. No prayer, looks as if someone should have prayed twenty-five years ago. I'll accept what I see but I need answers now! How come if you are my kin you never told me as much, in all the cards and gifts I've received from you in all these years? Girls listen, Tacy said. I made a promise to your Mother on her death bed, my Sister .yeah that's right, my Sister. My only Sister. Yes, I am your Aunt. I did the right thing. If you all would let me start from the beginning, the what, where and how.

Maybe I can explain. First let me call for some breakfast, I'll have it delivered. Cheese Omelets and toast O.K for everybody.

Not waiting for an answer Tacy called and ordered. The Clones waited in silence trying to figure out their lives. Nobody said a thing for ten minutes as the door-bell rang scaring the living shit out of all four. That must be breakfast. let's seat ourselves at the breakfast nook. It's in the back pass the solarium. I'll join you all in a second. One of you set the table, orange juice is in the frig.

They each walked back following directions to where Tacy led them feeling for their lockets. They each had them tucked away in different places on their persons. They ate in silence. Ok Torese spoke, we ate, we pretended, now it's time for some facts. She pushed her plate to the center of the table banging it against her Aunt Tacy's orange juice glass. She looked at Tacy hard.

Explain lady. Tia and Tangela both banged their glasses into Tacy's orange juice glass making it spill over. Ok lady enough bullshit the other two said together. Explain.

Aunt Tacy swallowed her remaining food. Wiped her mouth and stood up over them and pointed at Tia.

You Tia young lady. I see you are the first born and the most stubborn. Once I set you straight, I figured that other two clones will follow. Let me clear something up now. My name is not lady. Its Aunt Tacy to the three of you. If either of you ever talk to me in the tone I just heard. You will find yourselves picking each other up from a floored position.

Understand? No clone spoke. Now here's the truth. I am your Aunt. Accept it or not. I am to be respected in my house. She hit her fist on the coffee table hard. The only lesson to be learned here in my house today is that. This is my house! I've always sent my obligations through the mail and I've never sought either of you. I was forbidden.

Understand? They stared in awe not being able to speak.

Tacy continued. I have without a doubt in my mind fulfilled my peace with myself and my late Sister. I will be damned now twenty-five years later that I will let either of you control our first or final conversation. I'll teach each of you that my enemies never worry about me. They know where I stand. I believe family will be the first to fuck you. You don't want to fuck with me. I'll bring each of you down lower than a snake slivers on desert sand. She slammed her fist down on the table again. This time hard enough to make all their orange juice glasses fall off the table pouring out the contents on her plush carpet.

Did I make myself clear? No one said a word. The room was so quiet they could hear each other's lungs pumping air. Good, ok I'll continue. My parents, your Grandparents were born in Florence Italy. They survived the European war between nineteen hundred fourteen through nineteen hundred eighteen. In nineteen twenty-two they migrated to New York City. Their movement at that time was crushed by Mussolini's famous March on Rome. My parents spoke little English when they arrived in New York.

They made ends meet by selling illegal Whiskey while learning English at the same time. Years later they brought a store front property with their earnings from their illegal booze. One thing led to another. Shit happened, gambling, prostitution. Name it and they either sold it or had a hand in it. Nineteen thirty-nine I was born. four years later my Sister, your Mother came along.

By nineteen fifty everything fell apart. I think I was eleven your Mother maybe seven. Our parents survived the second war only to fall prey to New York immigrant's worst enemy. Ignorance and poverty. Then things really started to get bad. Papa started to drink heavy. Their business fell apart. The depression came upon us. The customers were poor, that meant no money for us.

My Papa died from either lack of faith or liver failure. The next year Mama died. She died from, let's see how should I put this, exhaustion from working two jobs or just plain giving up. I guess you can call giving up exhaustion also. I think maybe Mama knew once she died the two jobs would be no longer. Listen to me, I shall not repeat myself. Not only death could relieve my mother from worrying about her children. We all know worrying about one's kids is a full time job in itself. I think she thought dying was a way to get some rest. Tia, Tangela and Torese sat trance like hearing their beginnings for the first time. They listened, biting their nails sitting as still as statues. Once in a while they tilted their heads up in space to take in what their Aunt Tacy was saying. They lived the conversation. Aunt Tacy noticed their nervousness.

Can I get anyone anything to wet their tongues? Tia took the straight forward. Yes, I'll have anything straight as long as its strong. Tall glass no ice. Aunt Tacy's eyes shot across at her. Get it yourself. Sister Tangela can I offer you anything? No thank you, I'm fine. How about you Torese? I'll take a white wine please if you have any. Yes, honey I've got anything you want. I'll be pleased to join you. Tacy rose and fixed her and Torese a white wine in a very exquisite glass. She handed it to Torese without looking at Tia.

Tia smacked her lips making a loud sound. She got up and made herself a tall whiskey double no ice. Trying to provoke spike, provoking nothing. Aunt Tacy continued. Where was I? She walked over to the bar and stood beside Tia making Sister Tangela the most perfect Ice Tea. She handed it to the Sister and began again. After that your mother and I were turned over to social services. As I remember it we spent most of our time in offices while adults talked about our fate. We had nothing. We stayed with foster folks mostly Italian immigrants who knew our parents. All their friends tried to lend a helping hand. It was rough but my sister and I were together.

I protected my little sister hell or high water. Up times and down. God was always with us because we knew separation would have been devastating for the two of us. Without God we couldn't have stayed together. When I turned fifteen we were living with a foster family in a small apartment up the street from the subway and the empire state building. I doubt if some tenements still exist now, or maybe they do.

It was somewhere between seventy fourth and seventy fifth avenue on thirty first street or second street

Mirrored Injustice

I believe. Anyway the Empire State building was not far from where we stayed.

The couple we were with at that time really didn't care a lot for us. As long as they were responsible for us they received extra powdered milk, cheese, and spam. Surplus gave it. Social Services had seen to it that my sister and I received it. That period was the longest time we spent in one place. I think we stayed there three years. We left in nineteen fifty-seven. I was eighteen. Tacy breathed a long breath. Teauna was her name. My sister, your mother. Teauna Picenza. I changed my name to Peruvian when I lost her. Tacia Picenza is what I was born with. At eighteen we were sent to a Catholic Church in Philadelphia to stay with some nuns. Tacy faced Sister Tangela now. Yes, Tandy your mother and I stayed at the same convent you grew up in. We nicknamed you Tandy. I'll call you that now. Sister sounds a bit corny now with you being in my house and all. Don't speak let me finish my story. Tey and I stayed there until we got on our feet. Mom and I called her Tey from a baby, I couldn't pronounce her name for a long time. We were Tey and Tacy. Tey your mother was always different. Mellow and quiet. She kept her thoughts to herself confiding in me only after our parents died. I think she thought I was her reason for exiting. In all the places we lived, she hardly ever spoke.

I led, she followed. Sometimes with a nod or a blink. She was so delicately beautiful soft, and shy.

Aunt Tacy started to bite her nails nervously wringing her hands. She was so delicate at times that protecting her came naturally with my instincts.

The people we lived with before the church were name Scuzzi. They migrated with my parents and later changed their name to Scott. Anthony and Arita. Aunt Tacy licked her lips. The Scotts were good people in their hearts. When I turned eighteen they thought I could handle things, being the only one Tey spoke to and all. They trusted me to handle things and they turned us out.

She Arrita started to have many babies. After the Scotts we stayed at the convent for two years. I was twenty then, Tey sixteen. Social Services stepped in again giving us a check every month for two hundred dollars. And a room at the nearest Y.M.C.A. Neither of us were nun material. Sorry Tandy.

I took a job at the Y teaching swimming lessons to the underprivileged. Tey was at my side at all times. I learned to swim fast and perfect early on. If only I could remember from whom. It doesn't matter now. She lit a cigarette grabbing Tia's whiskey using it for an ash tray. No pun intended she said. All booze is over now. It's time for everyone to listen up. She flicked her ashes into Tia's glass. We oh let's see. Where was

Mirrored Injustice

I.

I was a good swimmer, my sister Tey a good listener. She read a lot. Her goal was school which made me pretty happy. She loved to experiment with things. She once told me she wanted to be a scientist. Anyway while I taught swimming lessons, I fed us and clothed us barely. When I saved enough money I sent Tey to future school. That's what it was called in those days. We may have lived at the Y, but Social Services seen to it again that as long as one of us stayed in school and continued our education we were entitled to collect Social Security checks. I don't know how. Our parent never really worked legally in the states. Maybe our Mom did for a short while at some point. Anyway I never completed my education but I had my job teaching swimming. As long as Tey stayed in school the checks came in along with my salary. We received seventy five dollars and sixty cents every third of the month. School was Tacy's life. She loved to experiment. Excuse me ladies, I hate to admit this but experimenting was what brought you clones in this world. We never took out a student loan for her, thank goodness. I'd probably be still paying it back. We lived on Tey's checks, my swimming salary and the Grants I applied for her to get. She received a Grant every time I filled out the papers for one. We must have read about and sought and filled out every single Grant that was available.

Tacy's throat was dry now. It was her turn to have cotton mouth. She licked her lips. Listen girls, I could go on forever. Does anyone want lunch or brunch. No please carry on Sister Tangela spoke. Ok I'll finish as much as I can. I may reveal to you three some things that may be disturbing to your minds. I'm caught between a hard place and Rocky Mountain. Sorry Tia, I know that's where you grew up. Listen girls if I continue. Your feelings may hit the fan and frankly I'm ready for my afternoon nap, maybe some lunch first. Maybe it would be best if we continued this later. Torese shocked herself. No Aunt Tacy, you've started so finish. Tia followed. Lady you put ashes in my glass so I suggest you continue while I make me another drink. She walked towards the bar. When she spoke she never looked her opponents directly in their eyes. Ok Aunt Tacy said to all three looking towards the bar to see low many fingers Tia's drink would measure.

She now needed sober Clones to drop this bomb shell. Girls I hope I get this right. If I don't I have a complete diary of everything upstairs in my safe.

I may even have some pictures. Sister Tandy started to relax. Pictures, I can go for some pictures.

Tacy knew the pictures would be her trump card. Now she sat back and watched their reactions. They were the identical Clones that she imagined they would always be. My sister Tey somehow lost faith in me. Am I repeating myself? Excuse me, anyway one of Tey's friends got her to participate in some kind of test tube bullshit. That was at the end of Nineteen sixty-three, the hippie era. Tey was in a strange state of mind. I know longer had any control over her. Her major was Science. Chemistry and lab were her best subjects. I wasn't in on the actual experiment. That's the year we lost communication or should I say Tey stopped trusting and confiding in me. As she got older and more beautiful she decided it was she instead of us. Her friends became her confidants. I couldn't say I knew what was going on then or now but, the more I talk about it the more it's starting to come back to me.

Listen girls, I'm ravenous and tired. The phone number to the restaurant that delivers, is in the book beside the phone. One of you call, I'm going to lay down for a while, call me when the food arrives. Not giving them time to protest again. Aunt Tacy exited to her room.

Norway Landed in Hawaii he felt the past through his briefcase, which he held on to tightly reminiscing the conversation of his latter boss. He was straight, serious and plenty sincere. He knew this trip was mandatory according to him, he had already conquered his goal thus far. He had finally surpassed the Godfather; the briefcase was his last obstacle. The girl in his briefcase was the last person to ever fuck with him in a condition of these sorts. His thoughts out ran his mind as he walked through the tunnel in the airport's terminal not sure where he was going. The girl in his briefcase became his obsession.

Father George Jessup was also among the ones that exited through the tunnel at the airport. He scurried along feeling his way not knowing where he was going, thanking God that the Holy Mother Mary sent him on this journey. Once he obtained the information she sent him to get, he would have her. Having her became his life goal but not the reason for him dedicating his life to the Monastery.

He'd had the chance to become the Abbott in his devotions but, he skipped that phase of his life wanting Mother Mary badly. Here now walking through the tunnel. Intact was his word for the day. The word made his dream a reality. If he didn't want to go back after the job was done. He wouldn't.

The girl in his briefcase wasn't to remain intact after their first encounter.

He walked towards the nearest light beyond the tunnel clenching his briefcase. He was sure this journey was produced by God.

Beyond Torese's wildest dreams, she could never have imagine Mike trying to find her after her absence.

Mirrored Injustice

For the first time in his life he put his job second, controlling Reese became his main goal. Losing that control meant defeat. He left his children with his brother's girlfriend who was the ultimate playgirl. They knew each other for at least a week. That didn't matter now he was on a mission to control his wife. Even if that meant hurting her once he found her. So be it. What ever happened to Reese's children, now it was her fault. He rode on the riding, moving, sidewalk thinking how he would love to put his hands around her neck. He dropped his briefcase for a split second. Retrieved it and turned around to see who was looking at him

Mike walked on straight out of the Hawaiian airport.

The Clones woke up Aunt Tacy with food. She rose in a lively mood. Please girls let's not turn into bitches. I would like to hear from you all. Tia, I'll start with you. Tell me about yourself. I want to hear about your life from the beginning up to now. I think you two girls would be interested also. Tia got into her mood. It only took a second. The stage was finally hers. Thanks, I'm a sucker for conversation. Should I play make pretend or address this mother fucking situation in the stinking way it was addressed to me? Ok Tia, that was your turn, let's go on. Tandy what about you? Aunt Tacy spoke, Ok lady, I'll play your fucking game. Don't cut me off. Tia voice spoke over everybody's. According to me and my

77

so call Mother and Father, I was reared in a small resort town called Aspen. Not Aspirin Ok? Nobody said a thing.

You asked me to tell you my story, my life. I'm really in the mood now. I don't mean to be disrespectful. I feel something coming of me now that I need to express, I'm gonna say it. Thanks for giving me the chance.

I've always felt different and strange since I was a little girl. Please don't get me wrong. I love my parents. My Mom and Dad is and will always be special to me. I have one Grandparent. That's Grands Morgan. I've always loved her, I just didn't like her. Matter of fact I hated the ground she thought her feet were too good to walk on.

Now that the truth is being forced upon me. I understand why Grands Morgan never liked me or my face sucking up her atmosphere. My folks been jet setting since I was born. I've had the best nanny's housekeepers, cooks and gardeners. All the people that was paid to upkeep me. We had a lot of houses. I've been around the world twice. Once when I graduated from high School, and the last time I went was for my Grands sake.

She decided I wasn't good enough and ordered my folks to send me away. She controlled everything and everyone that came into contact with her.

Mirrored Injustice

I've had tutors since I can remember. Grands paid for it all. Now I really know why she never thought I was good enough for anything. She always said since I started kindergarten that Aspen schools were too good for me. She said I belonged in the ghetto.

I have no problem living in the ghetto, if that's the life God gave me, but I do thank God I'm alive every moment. If I didn't make anything of my life thus far, I would be worse off than I am now. I'm glad to know for the first time in my life today that I'm not related to that miserable old bitch. My Mother, Tacy shot her a strange look and Tia corrected herself. I do love her but now I see and understand why she did what she did. My Mother and my Grandmother treated me like shit. I often wondered why Mom and Dad never stood up to Grands, why they never told her where to get the fuck off. Tia started to cry trying not to show her tears. She wiped them with her sleeve quickly. I went to school in Aspen all my life. Kindergarten, Middle and High School. Twelve years.

After I graduated, Grands had Mom and Dad enroll me into Harvard. I lasted a month. When it finally came to end, my college days, dad flew up and got me. We flew back to Aspen together. He told me on the plane. Toy, he called mc that to this day. He said, Toy when we land, Grands would like to talk to you.

Cookie Johnson Grant

My Dad could never handle his Mother and when he called me Toy he stuttered. Toy always came out as ba boy. My Mom never ever told me what to do. God I hated that old lady. When I dropped out of Harvard my dad and I arrived in Aspen. Tia sniffed and wiped her nose on her sleeve. We didn't go to our home, we went straight to Grands house.

Mom was a blue lady at the hospital. She volunteered her time to others to keep herself significant. We hardly ever talked. My Dad and I were close. I remember he used to joke with me and say that if I did what Grands told me and didn't anger her that he would give me two hundred dollars. So I got two hundred dollars every week and I wasn't supposed to tell my mother. So I got my weekly allowance from her too. He told me that all girls my age obeyed their Grands at my age and one day I would inherit the earth. I thought that maybe he wanted her to die and leave everything to her only Granddaughter.

I was as good as gold to the old bitch. Tia sniffed. I thought if I be good I would inherit the earth and when I did, I would give it to my Dad because he deserved it.

He was the reason I was being good. I guess I was wrong. I lived a life as a lie. I am not that woman's Granddaughter. She knew it, that's why she treated me like she treated me.

Mirrored Injustice

Tia got up and walked over to the bar. Aunt Tacy paid her no attention at this point, she only wanted her to get on with the story. Tia went on. Grands read me the worthless act for failing leaving Harvard.

Tia fixed her a strong drink and continued to talk. I listened to her tell me what a failure I was because that's what I was taught to do. There were times when she made me feel like the garbage in her disposal. Dad never said one word. Grands made me cry as usual. Once I couldn't control my tears I knew I wasn't about to let Grands cause me to have a nervous breakdown. Even if I knew my dad was having a silent one. I politely said fuck you, lady and walked out. That's the night I met the Cobra Tia sighed, inhaled, took a breath letting her last sentence flow as if she had a respiratory problem.

She breathed deeply. This story is sickening. I don't know why I started it. I'm not talking anymore. She walked toward the bar and poured the vodka again in her drink turning her back toward them.

Aunt Tacy gave Tia no sympathy. She didn't let her in her mind one way or another. Ok Tandy she dismissed Tia at the bar knowing she was getting more than drunk. Tangela I would like to hear about you. I know you came from the convent. I think it's time you let us real relatives hear about just what makes you the person that came to me today.

Sister Tangela Mancini looked down at her stolen coveralls feeling a terrible sadness. I really don't know where to begin she said holding her head down. She looked around her and her eyes started to water. How can I be in form to tell my story honestly? I'm wearing stolen clothes. Aunt Tacy handed her the Kleenex box. Tandy honey your clothing being stolen shouldn't bother you if you know in your heart that you are a good person. Honey sometimes we all has to do things in order to survive. Be strong honey now for all our sakes.

In order for us to go on now we have to familiarize each other with where we've been so we can know how to continue. We've got a long journey to go. Sister Tangela Mancini took control of herself.

I've been an orphan all my life. She spoke with a vengeance. I've lived in a religious environment since I was found abandoned and raped at five.

Everything before that I have no knowledge of. Thank God. Mother Mary and Father Jessup taught me how to eject such thoughts from my mind. They told me that the only way my soul could reach purity. What a joke! I rinsed my mind and cleansed my soul for many years, of anyone that wasn't Godly. I was raised with strict religion. It was like, she blew her nose. I thought I didn't have a choice.

Mirrored Injustice

Somewhere deep down inside I've always felt that there was a person dying to come out. And how I rejected those feelings and now I'm falling apart.

I want to say the f word so bad now I can taste it. I've wanted to say that word since I can remember. I've never had the guts. Fuck, fuck, fuck. Now I said it. Am I so much a bad person? They all stared at her but nobody said a word. I guess I'm in real trouble with God, should I go on? Sure honey it's your turn speak your peace Aunt Tacy said. My peace, funny you would refer to this as my peace. I never had any fucking peace. There I said it again. Excuse me. I've never said that word before and I must say I feel good. I came from what I considered a loving parent.

Mother Mary my superior loved me every step of the way. Must I continue on with this Aunt Tacy? I'd rather not if it's Ok with you. Its ok honey I understand. What about you Torese? Want to fill us in on what you've been up to till now? Yeah why not she said scooting down to the edge of her seat. But call me Reese. Let's see how should I begin? I come from very loving parents. They adopted me before I was a year old. They couldn't conceive but lo and behold after the got me along came three more homemade ones. Since then I sort of been on my own. In their own way they loved me I suppose, but every word one of their monsters breathed or spoke was took to be the genuine absolute honest to

83

god fucking truth without a doubt. My parents never hid the fact that I was the adopted one. That was Ok with me considering the monsters they birthed. I never expected anymore then what I got. Anyway my siblings made the word adopted a word I love to hate, when they said the word I used to cringe, that mere word sent shivers and chills through me. Always leaving me with a terrible migraine. I used to run as fast as I could to my room to get away from them. Mom and Dad always said I was the one who enjoyed being by myself, which I did because they never disciplined their monsters all they ever said was for me to grow up and stop being so emotional. So my first year of high school I met Mike. He fucked my brains out, turning me into the person him and his family thought I should be. Stupid and pregnant. I waited on that bastard from the first second I laid my eyes on him up until a few days ago. The only thing he ever gave me besides physical pain and emotional heartache was three lovely children whom I sit here and ache for. My oldest two are twins, I've always wondered where that blessing came from. Nobody in Mike's family was more than one, less than one I might add. And my family well I just thought that somebody was blessed with twins. Now I know, don't I? Now that I sit here aching for my children I must tell you that I am in a mist of confusion that spell trouble.

Mirrored Injustice

Oh I forgot to mention my baby Mitchell who I miss most of all. Her eyes watered.

I am a battered wife and now that everybody sitting here know all my troubles, I'll leave it at that for now. Ok girls, I appreciate all of your honesty. Now I want you perfect pretty clones to listen to me. Focus all your energies and personalities on me for now. Together maybe we can fix each other's problems or anything else that needs to be fixed. As long as we can agree on the method of how we fix it. Everybody's dilemma is everybody's, we need to mend each other's lives now.

What we really need to do now is think. Think deeply. We all can use each other's help. Our main goal should be where do we go from here. And the place we need to be at is incognito with each other. Which by my definition is a group hug. All rise. Let's stand and hug the nearest person to each other. Let's cry it out, I know I have more to cry about then anyone in this room. Come on ladies lets cry. Aunt Tacy and her Clones stood, hugged and cried together. Their tears flowed for the umpteenth time. They group hugged and cried. Then cried some more.

Its funny how what goes around usually comes back smacking the shit out of folks as it now did the three jerks that left the airport together each seeking a girl but for all different reasons. Fate somehow ended the trio up together. They got drunk, drinking to their stomachs became content in the nearest bar. Being content was not what either three was there for.

Buy these mother fuckers a drink on me Mike Mehan roared at the top of his lungs pointing at Father Jessup and Norway. Norway interrupted just as drunk as the two of them. No man the drinks are on me. Please Mr. Bartender give all my new friends a drink. Company's expense. He burst into laughter lying his ass off. Norway, the Father and Mike were indeed in each other's company. All riding on the juices of the alcohol. I'm from California Mike slurred, where are you fellows from? He belched, excuse me I'm drunk. At least I'm drunk and having fun. They all roared and slammed their palms down on top of the bar. The Bartender eyeballed the trio with contempt. Come on fellows I know you have a mortgage somewhere fess up, Father Jessup laughed, the alcohol just introducing itself to his system for the first time since Sunday's wine. He liked it. This was hard alcohol giving him personality and spunk. I'm from Philadelphia. He was having a ball. I don't drink he stuttered laughing. I don't think I can drink anymore tonight Mike the more serious of the trio responded. Well I think I'll drink all night while I got this fucker paying at his company's expense.

All three laughed uncontrollable. Ok let's all get serious here, I know for a fact that neither of us is from here. Yeah the way the bartender is looking at us is a sure giveaway Mike said.

They roared with laughter again. Father Jessup lost his balance and toppled over onto the floor between the stools. Mike got down and picked him up from behind holding on to him from behind his rib cage. Mike's head begun to spin as he realized he could not hold on to the fellow or try to pick him up. Norway watched the two go down as he could hardly comprehend what was going on around him. He still tried to help. He fell on top of the drunk twosome.

The three woke up the next morning in a jail cell drunk tank literally sleeping on top of each other. Their breath stank, their clothes were wrinkled. Each of them had their belongings no matter how drank they'd gotten. Which was securely locked up in the jails safe. Norway was the first to free himself from the entanglement away from his newly drinking buddies. What the fuck, his words hurt his head, where the fuck am I?

Get the fuck off me mother fucker. Who the fuck are you two? Father Jessup was sincere and heaped his shoulders forward letting the two rise. He straightened up his clothing and stood up. I am George Jessup. There is no need for confusion or any need to be upset or use profanity. We all met last night.

I don't remember all the events, whatever we did we did it together or we three wouldn't be in this situation together now. Fix your clothing men, at least try to act like we know how we got here, even if it's just for the jailers sake. Mike and Norway stood and brushed their clothing downward, straightening their attire. Father Jessup took the assertive role making himself their leader without realizing it. Your name is Mike right? He pointed at one of the two men. Yeah right man, I also have three kids and a bitch for a wife, a dog and a mortgage and my life sucks. Do you know all that garbage too? Where and why the fuck am I here? I'm in fucking jail since you seem to know everything I guess I don't have to tell you that, do I mother fucker? Mike rubbed the back of his head. That was as far as he got before Father Jessup erupted loudly. Listen you sleaze bag, Father was in a hung over mood now and ready to take it out on the first person that gave him any reason too. That morning was the first time in his life he had ever been hung over.

I was not a mother fucker last night and this morning I won't be one either. According to you last night you needed me to be your friend if nothing else. Boy I think you have a lot of problems whether you choose to recognize them without being drunk or not is your problem. Not mine. Father Jessup stared directly in Mikes face.

Excuse me Mike spoke holding his ground. I don't seem to be able to remember shit that happened last night. As far as I'm concerned you both are a bunch of sleaze bag assholes that got me in this trouble. As soon as I get away from you two the better off I'll be. Whatever the reason I came here for is none of either one of your business so shut the fuck up. You can continue the argument later after I get myself out of this stupid situation Ok? Ah the poor man wants us to leave him alone that's not what you wanted last night. Father Jessup shot him a look that said shut up, I've got the floor now. He was on a role now. The last thing I remember last night before succumbing to this predicament I'm in now is that we were all trying to find out where each of us resides. I'll start fresh. Hello, my name is George Jessup. I'm only here for one reason.

I'm from Philadelphia. In my heart I know I should treat you both as children because that's what I'm used to dealing with. If that's how you act, that's how I'll treat you. Who are you? Where do you come from and why do you think you are in jail with me?

Well George, I'm Norway woods. Norway took the incentive. Leaving Mike to be the asshole. I'm from Aspen Colorado he lied. I'm here for a reason. Mike was left out now looking like a ass by his two new comrades. Don't ask me any questions, and please don't talk to me. I don't know either of you two and I'm happy with that. Mike grabbed the only pillow in the cell and laid back down and covered his head. He spoke muffled from underneath the pillow like a toddler. I'm Mike Mehan and I'm on a fucking mission. They each heard footsteps and keys jingling and they heard the lock turn. Mike Mehan, George Jessup, Norway Woods, front and center, all of you.

The jailers read their names from each of their driver's license, returning them to them as they exited past the jailer. Sorry about last night the jailer said. Your Honor was out of town, he's back now and what I've written about you three, you'll be lucky to get out of here now. Follow me. All three men without looking at each other followed the guard without a word. They found out that the judge posted a thousand-dollar bail for each individual meaning they each had to pay a hundred dollars to get out of there. They were charged each with disorderly conduct, disturbing the peace and resisting arrest. Neither man was in any mood or condition to resist anything now, they left the jail house exiting faster than they entered. Once they got outside they realized at the same time that they had no transportation. Mike the most spoiled of the three threw his hands up. Ah fuck, he turned to the two new friends of his. How did I get here or do either of you two know?

I believe we rode in a paddy wagon, Father Jessup said. Our rent a cars must be where we left them, parked at the bar. Anybody interested in splitting a cab? Mike looked at him. You remember where the bar is? No not

really but I bet one of those jailers does. Father turned
going back into the building. Get a load of that fucker
Mike said to Norway. Yeah Norway answered what
planet did he drop off of? Norway looked at Mike
strangely wondering if he could be trusted. I don't
remember anything about last night He said rubbing his
temples trying to relieve the ache that made looking
through his eyes miserable. I remember somebody
talking about being on a mission. Are you on a mission?
Maybe Mike answered.

Are you. Yeah I know I am but my head hurts.
Let's say, we stick together closely and solve our
missions together? What you got to say about that?
Maybe. Maybe shit Norway said do you know anyone
here? No and neither do I.

I remember more of what you said last night then
you realize I do. So please don't fucking try me. What
hotel are you staying in?

Mike said boldly, I'm not staying in no fucking hotel
here where the fuck are you staying. You tell me first
where your hotel is, Mike gritted his teeth used to being
the aggressor with Reese and used to getting his way.

Norway gritted his teeth also. I didn't get a hotel yet
man. I came straight from the airport to that bar. Yeah I
did too. They chucked together for the first time sober.
Wanna share the expenses for lodgings together?
Norway spoke. Mike responded I already spent one

night with you in tight quarters, I suppose I can survive just about anything now. Father Jessup swung the double glass doors open coming outside to join the two men with the address of the bar where they left their rent a car.

We're on our way he says full of life as he usually was. Norway and Mike eyeballed each other as they walked down the steps of the jail exiting it. They swung their eyes at each other as they hailed a cab.

After the teary scene at Aunt Tacy's. All the Clones decided to come clean. They each told of the events that led them to Hawaii. Then to Kaho'olawe. Aunt Tacy asked for a description of the two men that followed Tia out of Aspen's airport. After hearing that Tia secured the briefcase on herself once she verified that there was indeed five million dollars in it. Aunt Tacy, Reese, Tia, and Tandy looked at Reese's snapshots from her wallet. Aunt Tacy then made a mental note of what Mike looked like. Knowing the men chasing Tia would have to eventually come her way. She also got a description of what Mike looked like from Reese's wallet just in case.

Tacy decided the Sister was probably the safest one since no one but the police would be looking for her. At least her life wasn't in danger. Aunt Tacy made a few phone calls putting the word out in all the local bars for all to be on the alert. All was left to do now was to wait.

Mirrored Injustice

They didn't wait long. The phone rang. Tacy spoke quietly, then she hung up. She turned and looked at the three Clones. There were three men together last night at the Cantina. One fits the description of your husband Reese.

Would he bring along friends? I doubt it Aunt Tacy. He doesn't have any. He hid his abusiveness well. If he's here that must mean my children are with lord knows who. I pray they're o.k. They must be fine Aunt Tacy said sympathetically. We must concentrate on finding out who the other two men are, with your husband. I'll make some more calls. She learned from Myia Kwan the owner of the Palm tree hotel that the three men she was looking for were registered in Myia's abode. Only after three phone calls.

Aunt Tacy hung up the phone and read the names to her clones hoping for a response.

Mike Mehan, George Jessup and Norway Woods. Anyone recognize the names beside Reese. Reese that's your husband Mike Mehan right? Sister Tangela's eyes widened with fear. Aunt Tacy. George Jessup is my Father Jessup. He runs the Monastery; He is the Abbot. He lives not far from my Convent. He is my Mother Mary's good friend. I wonder why he's here, wait a minute Aunt Tacy said, this means that the police is not yet involved with your situation. Maybe I should call Mother Mary Tandy said. Maybe you should but now let's figure this thing out first. Let's find out who the other man is first. Then we all will make the call. Does anyone of you know who Norway is? No one spoke. Tia you're the only one who's left. Do you recognize the name? Sorry Aunt Tacy I never heard it before. Tia sobered up really fast now wanting to participate in the conversation, and be a part of them for the first time without her smart mouth.

Ok then let's get some sleep. Tomorrow I'll go to the bank and then I'll do some shopping for some clothes for you girls to wear while you're here. In the meantime, I want you clones to look just as you do now. When I return I want to see the perfect clones I left. Make yourselves look exactly like the mirror images sitting in front of me now. Sister Tandy your hair is the shortest. Tia and Reese, I guess you two should cut you hair to Tandy's length. When I return from shopping, I don't want to be able to tell who's who. Not that I can now.

I don't really want to cut my hair Tia said. If my, I mean our plan is going to work you must do as I say. The three of you must look exactly alike to everyone including me if we're going to fix this situation Tia. I never really had a chance to do anything besides send things through the mail so now I have my chance and I'm going to do it right. I'll blow anyone out of the water that think their smart enough to come after one of my Clones. Must you refer to us as your Clones? Tia said

94

going towards the bar again. I don't like the phrase. You got a better analogy? Never mind don't answer there's no time to fight over petty things I got a better suggestion. Tia you ever handled a gun before? Yeah my Dad took me hunting every year since I was four. Remember I was born and raised in Aspen. I know how to shoot very well thank you. Got a gun, want me to show you? One year I shot a elk before my Dad got the chance to aim at him. Good you come with me, Tandy and Reese if you're tired you can retire if you want, we won't be long. They left Tandy and Reese stretching and yawning on the couch while they walked out the door and around the corner to Tacy's shop. I guess you enjoy telling fortunes? Tia said.

Yes, I do, why do everything you said have to sound so sarcastic? Do you believe what you tell those poor stupid people to be truthful? Yes, I do, why? Cause I think you talk a bunch of bullshit, excuse my French. That's your opinion Tia and you are entitled to it. Ok since that's my opinion do you know what the future holds for us three clones as you so delicately call us. Well I see you changing your ways after the life you lived up to now. And I see you reaching a place in your life to not be so taken by material things, am I right? Bullshit lady see I knew you didn't know what you're talking about. I've never been about material things before I came here and nothing you have impresses me.

It's all your opinion and your opinion only. Aunt Tacy took a deep breath. Ok I guess then that your Grands Morgan can't possibly have an opinion about you and the contents of that briefcase that I didn't invite to my house. Isn't money the most wanted material on earth?

Tia felt like she was in a sinking ship but she refused to show it. Her eyes squinted and her jaws clenched. So you think you know Grands well do you considering that I never saw you before in her presence and do you always snoop through the things of your guest? Well honey I think you don't know what you talk about either because the definition of guest is someone you invite to invade your space where ever it be. Agree? Well Grands just jealous of me because she's old. Tia started to regress to her childhood knowing that her ship had sank.

I doubt that child, she is just as wise as she is old. A mother only wants to do what is best for her child and her child is a man that you didn't know had adopted you and she did. And by the way how come you failed to mention the briefcase in your introduction? Because I thought that was none of your business. You made it my business when you brought it into my home. How much money would you say is inside it? I don't know I haven't gotten around to counting it yet. Well since I'm the fortune teller I'll tell you. Its close too five million dollars all in hundred dollar unmarked bills. Where'd you get it? I took it from the assholes that's chasing me. And that's even more reason I bought you out here Aunt Tacy said starting to soften. The gun. I'm leaving early in the morning to do some shopping for you three. I need you, I think you're the strongest of my clones, oops excuse me, my niece. Lady not to change the subject but. Tia please don't call melady I prefer Tacy or I'd really love Aunt Tacy. Ok Aunt Tacy, I'd prefer your nieces instead of your clones and Tia instead of girl or honey, truce? Yes, we have a truce. That's what I only wanted from you since I got to know your personality. I love you. Now that you didn't want to change the subject and we're getting to like each other change it, I dare you. Ok I will Tia said realizing for once that she wanted to like this person and respect her ways. What do you think of my two new sisters? I think, they're a bit boring don't you?

Well I know them as well as I know you Aunt Tacy said, and I don't find you boring, I find all three of you fascinating and I'm glad you finally came my way. Now let's get to the gun, I'm tired, I have a long day tomorrow. Here load this. She handed her a silver hand gun. Know what Aunt Tacy, Tia said taking the small silver gun and the gold tip bullets. This gun fits your personality perfectly. It's pretty enough to fool any ten-year-old. What'll you mean by that Aunt Tacy said curiously well it looks play. Well too damn bad it's not play and you're not a ten-year-old.

Let's see your stuff, load it. Tia loaded the gun with expertise, cocked it and aimed it at the mirrors strutting her stuff posing then gently unloaded it and handed it back to Aunt Tacy. How's that? That's good, you do know what you're doing but remember it's not a toy. I'm leaving you to be the protectors of your sisters. Why, because you think their wimps? Tia said being honest with her Aunt. I never said that, I choose you to handle the gun because I figured you had the training for it, living in Colorado and being the only one to have a Dad that lived there all his life. I just figured with hunting and all.

Do me a small favor, when I'm gone tomorrow promise me, no booze. Ok? You think that I'm drunk? Well I think I can handle things with or without booze, my choice. Listen Tia, see you tempt me to call you girl but I didn't, I said no booze while there's a gun in my house, understand? And if you don't understand or see why, you can leave through the same door you entered. You're not ten and it's about time you started acting like the lady you are. Maybe you are an alcoholic. Don't piss me off, I can cross the line between loving you and tolerating you. Your choice. ok. Ok lady I get it you don't have to get hot under the collar. Tacy glared at her. What's my name? They were standing eye to eye contact now. Call me lady one more time an I'll show you the door. What's my name? Ok its Tacy, Tia said with a lump welding up in her throat wondering why this lady was doing her like this. I can't hear you Tacy said without moving a muscle in her entire body, but her mouth. Give me the respect I'm due. Ok Aunt Tacy, Tia said matter of fact. What do you want me to say? How do you want me to act? Should I keep on repeating your name over and over would that be my punishment? Tears rolled down her face. Is that what you wanted to hear? I think you take pleasure in making people cry. Tacy walked away from her heading out of the shop and Tia followed without the pistol. Get the gun Tia and God forbid you're not to let it out of your sight ever again.

Aunt Tacy strutted, clapped her hands as she entered seeing the other two Clones were not asleep but still sitting on the couch. We're back and since you're still up we might as well get down to business. Write me down some sizes, looks like you're all about the same size. Anyway, Tia will be in charge of the door and the phone tomorrow when I go shopping. You two cut each other's hair and take charge of the cooking. When I return, I expected a decent meal. Oh, and watch Tia, she is not to have any alcohol while I'm gone. And lock the door behind me tomorrow morning as soon as I leave. Well ladies I'm going to bed now, I'm tired. I suggest you three do the same.

The next day Tacy went to the bank and withdrew five thousand dollars ignoring the hundreds she'd seen in Tia's briefcase. That was strictly Tia's choice to decide what was to be done with its contents Tacy thought. Now she was going to spoil them rotten. This was the first time she had a chance to pay her dead sister back for being in her life and leaving her with such beautiful Clones,

Unconsciously she enjoyed Tia's spunk to say whatever emotion reached her brain at the time it reached it. Tia reminded her of her dead sister, Tacy shielded the thought from her mind. That was her other life.

She pulled up after a long days shopping in front of her garage in her Mercedes using her remote control she entered the house through her kitchen with both arms loaded with bags and boxes. To her surprise all three clones were showered, each with robes on and towels wrapped around their heads. Lasagna was in the upright oven as one of them poked at it. Another was cutting up vegetables and another was washing the dishes and wiping the counter tops as fast as her helpers would leave droppings. Tacy thought if she didn't know their individual personalities by now she probably would never get the hang of it. She couldn't tell one from the other. All was perfect. Hello whoever you are. Dinner smells good. Thanks. I need a hand with the rest of the things in the car. She didn't give them an inch, her father used to say to her mother about her and her sister, give them an inch, they will take a yard. That instant she understood who they were, the children she never had. Torese and Tangela both wiped their hands dry and went to help get the bags from the car. Tia kept tending to the Lasagna never letting her personality wavier for a second, that's how Tacy knew who she was. How was shopping Aunt Tacy? Putting an empathize on the words Aunt Tacy. Was shopping for us a delight? Tacy made a mental note of her movements to remember her as an individual to be dealt with. Shopping was fun but my feet hurt, how was your day? Do you know who I am? Tia said knowing that she finally did exactly like she was told and it was backfiring on her Auntie. Yeah, you're Tia and you think I'm stupid. Tangela and Torese came in the kitchen door from the garage with more bags then they could carry. And that's Tandy and Reese with all the goodies. Pretty good for a stupid Aunt huh Tia, Tacy said taking off her shoes and rubbing her feet while holding on to the kitchen table. I think we got it all Sister Tangela said shyly without looking her Aunt directly into her eyes. Tacy thought my next project looking at the shy lamb, what a job. Tandy come with me. Tia and Reese bring the bags up to my room please, Tandy and I will sort them and could you bring us up some of that good smelling dinner when its ready?

Thanks that will give me and Tandy some time to get to know each other a little better. Tandy grab some bags and follow me. Tacy reached for a bag and headed for the staircase. Tandy did the same and the two others grabbed the remaining packages and followed. Tia thought to herself, this bitch must think this is the fucking Marines . Once upstairs Tia and Torese deposited all their packages on the bed and exited like the Clones Soldiers they were becoming. Tacy shut the door quietly behind them.

Tandy, Aunt Tacy said flopping down on the bed in the mist of all the packages. Help me sort these clothes out and then we can divvy them up. You're not tired are you? No not really, I'11 do anything to help. Just what Aunt Tacy thought silently to herself. I wasn't sure what to get for you. I know you were probably used to uniforms. How do you feel about jeans? I'll wear anything you've brought for me thanks for all your help and kindness, I'm grateful. Oh no need to be grateful Tacy said, it's my job now to take care of you now. Have you ever wore them before? No ma'am I haven't. The coveralls I have on now, I stole them. She looked at the floor. Look at me Tangela Picenza. Tandy looked her into her eyes for the first time. Why do you call me that? Because honey that was your name at birth. I need to know or at least try to figure out what happened to you between the time you were born and the time you said you entered the orphanage raped at five years old. I always thought you were in the hands of the Sisters since my sister Tey gave you up. Why didn't you take me Aunt Tacy? Why didn't you make me feel like I belonged to somebody like my two real sisters did? Tandy I want you to know, I think you deserve to know why I let the fate that became you happen to you, why I did what I did. Listen to me carefully. After the Genetic experiment your Mother participated in, she died as you were coming into this world. As her pregnancy progressed, towards the end she knew her destiny. She thought she was doing the right thing by protecting me and thinking of my happiness, she begged me not to take either of her children. Did my Mother know she was having more than one child? Yes, let the truth be known she knew exactly how many children the experiment could produce but not really knowing how many she would have.

And she knew near the end that there could be a possibility of her dying. Aunt Tacy did my Mother swear you to secrecy about all this or can you tell me about it? Only if you're ready to hear it. I'm ready more then you know, please tell. Me. Tandy with the problems you've come to me with I'm afraid that adding to them could be detrimental to your peace of mind. Aunt Tacy I'll be the judge of my peace of mind, your responsibility now is to set me free of any lack of information that comes along with learning to deal with my new life, and accepting my new family. I need to know what led up to you not being able to raise me and what part the experiment played in my sisters getting a better life than myself.

Why did you let me live a life that I've doubted and why now do I sit here and you show no remorse. I'm sorry you feel that way Tandy I do feel remorse but you sought me, I did not seek you.

Fuck who sought who Aunt Tacy I don't think that's the issue. See I'm learning fast and you know what? I enjoy using the fuck language and ill sorts of things, I'll tell you something else by golly, if I sit here and listen to you stall any longer I may seek anger after I 'vomit. I've already killed one person that could have been avoided if only you've had the courage to raise me after my Mother died. She started to cry. You know how that makes me feel? I feel like slapping the living shit out of you. Lady you gave me a raw deal. Tandy heaved, now that I've released my thoughts and my dirty words that only I have had to live with. I suggest you tell me what I want to know. Aunt Tacy clapped. That was a good lecture Sister girl for you being a nun and all. I'm glad you got it all out. This is going to be harder than I thought, I know you need answers and I'm proud to be the one that can give them to you but I'd rather get to know you first, come on let's talk one on one. Tandy's whole body swelled. How many people do you see in this room? Enough of this nonsense, nobody knows what I've been through, you tell me about my Mother and me now! She reached for a pair of scissors that was laying on top of the doily that circled beneath Tacy's perfumes on the vanity and yelled, TALK TO ME NOW

LADY! Whoa Sister girl calm yourself, do you really think I believe you have the guts to hurt me in my own house, and if you did have the guts, where would that leave you. Tacy talked tough, truly Tandy scared her. Now put down the scissors, before they turn up in your body during your autopsy. Tacy was extremely calm and spoke very low. I would never hurt you but I'm not going to let you hurt me, either. Tandy threw the scissors across the room and begun to sob hard. like an actress rehearsing for a scene she stopped suddenly as if she cut off her own breath. Her tears dried instantly. She turned her back to Aunt Tacy and stared into the mirror to the vanity.

Tandy began to count like a person truly possessed. One, two, three, four, five, six. Aunt Tacy felt sorry for her and gave in on a situation that was scary and needed to be dealt with delicately. Ok Tandy I'll tell you what you need to know. Stop counting please. I told you before that I have pictures and records to back up what I say. Turn around, look at me, let's get comfortable. You and your Sisters are all just alike.

Please never call me lady again. Ok here goes. My Sister your Mother was offered Twenty-five hundred dollars to participate in an experiment. In nineteen sixty-three that was a lot of money. The experiment she took place in was called MGB (Multiple Genetic Births.)

At the time, I didn't know much about it. The laboratory at the college, Tey was attending said they discovered a cure for females who couldn't have children, at that time they just couldn't figure out why. I know that now.

The college administrators at the lab said all they had to do was take this medication and report to them for follow ups every time they menstruated. I never knew the name of the medication. I was to ignorant I guess to pay attention to details as Tey tried to clue me in. She knew I was against it so she hesitated and left things out when she did bother to try to tell me about it. The administrators told them that they may or may not become pregnant. Tey lied for the money and told them she couldn't have children. They never bothered to check. She did tell me that the lab had willing participants lining the halls down three flights of stairs, out the door and around the corner.

She thought the twenty-five hundred dollars would get us a life out of the ghetto. I argued with her over and

over again. She was so pretty I told her that her prince
would eventually come along sooner or later and rescue
her from the life she seem to hate more than I did. Soon
or later never came. By me nagging her all the time she
stopped confiding in me completely. I found out the rest
from her friends and classmates after her death. I cried
and cried until I was blue in the face. Obviously not
enough beforehand.

When I realized the fact that my sister was going to
die, I had no control over it. I lost control of myself after
that and was not responsible enough to take care of
myself let alone three girls. I spent eighteen months in a
mental institution in New York. The college
administrators took sole responsibility for her funeral
and they buried her in a manner that I couldn't. They
also placed you three. She never got the money. By the
time I got better enough to investigate, it was too late to
do anything about it. They had long ago cleared
themselves of any evidence and all wrong doings.

She delivered five girls, two died at birth. Tandy I'm
sorry. I'm telling you the story, nothing but the truth.
Don't be sorry Aunt Tacy just continue to talk and be
honest. Who was our Father? How did the experiment
produce us without a male?

Your Father is another story in itself. He was Teys'
childhood friend. When our parents died there was a
boy about eight years old, His family made the journey

with us to the States. Our parents were best friends all their lives. They were a close wholesome foursome, we all lived together while our folks made illegal liquor and sold it. It stemmed back as far as Italy. Anyway after Mom and Dad died, the system took me and Tey. His parents ran away from him leaving him to fend for himself. I sort of took care of him up until the experiment. But after that I never saw him again. He never knew whether the experiment took or not. He and Tey never had sex, according to them.

If he's alive I'm sure that he doesn't know you three exist. He didn't stay around long enough to find out the outcome of the situation. Let me explain how it went. Every day before Teys lunch break she was injected with a medication mixed with your Father's sperm. He gave his sperm loyally. Nothing happened for a while. He was getting paid for his part in it a little at a time , but they told Tey that she couldn't get her money until she produced. He got money for his donations and when they finally gave him the rest in full. When the money exchanged hands, before we knew anything he'd already disappeared. I never saw him again. If he's still alive , I'm sure he knows nothing about you three, but I bet my life on it that he wonders about the outcome. Tandy interrupted. What was His nationality Aunt Tacy? Well that's the hard part. He came from Italy like we did but his Dad was a Black French man who migrated from

Mirrored Injustice

France because of the war. He was light dark with curly soft hair and he fell in love with a French girl. The two became my parents best friends. Tacy looked at Tandy for a response, she got none. She continued. They had a son, his name was Motzi He was your Father. He loved American money the first time he laid his eyes on it. We three were practically raised as brother and sisters until the tragedy gave us the fate that took us each to different lives. Money? he doesn't have a clue about you three. His family escaped from Italy with my family, I mean our family. All we knew then, was survival we were too young and too wanting for a life without war and pain to know anything about racism, thank God. Your Dad was a part of our family since he was born, So Tandy interrupted again, what does that make me? Tacy looked at Tandy taking her face into her hands, I could say a number of things but only you know for sure. Are you prejudice Tandy? I don't know and I come from the church. I've never had any contact with Black people before. I think Mother Mary was probably prejudice. She taught us to never hire anyone outside of our nature or faith. Well let me inform you of a very import lesson since that's what you've been taught so far. People come in all shades, and everyone is entitled to their own opinions so this is how I deal with situations of the delicate discriminating nature. When I meet a person for the first time, I give them a ten, I think everyone deserves at lease that much. At the time of introductions. In the time we get to know each other we may or may not like each other. They either become my friend and remain a ten or bring themselves down notch by notch until they reach zero.

Then, I don't want them breathing the same air space as I do.

The moral of the story is that don't judge people by what they look like on your first encounter, treat people by their personalities, and their potential to deal with you.

People are people, when we die were dead. There is no race yet that is the superior when it comes to who lives longer or who goes to a better place when we die. And if that ever happens and we are divided by race, I hope I am on the side that does the discovering, until then I'll just find my longevity within my own heart. I was not put here to judge others.

So what you say we include your sisters in on this conversation, I'm sure they would enjoy hearing it also. Then we can get on with whatever we need to do. That's fine with me, Tandy said wanting badly for her just to get on with the conversation. She felt warm and happy when Tacy spoke.

They all gathered on the bed and talked for a long time until they came to know each other and felt comfortable enough to laugh a little. Tacy felt she was getting to know them better. She was always on her guard watching and listening and wanting to savor every second with them. They ate the Lasagna and salad that the clones made for dinner and later Tacy served them cheese, crackers, grapes and wine. They ate, talked, and laughed and were very happy until the wee hours of the morning. Tia was checking out Aunt Tacy's wardrobe and as she reached into the closet, she accidentally turned off the bedroom light. That's when they realized it was day. They continued on with that sorts for three more days. Then the phone rang and broke their monotony .Hush girls Aunt Tacy said picking up the receiver trying to adjust the popcorn around in her mouth so she could speak properly. Hello, this is Tacy, your fortune is my pleasure, if it is in the cards I will find it, if I can't find it then it's not there. Are you calling to make an appointment? Is this Tacy Picenza? The voice on the other end said. Yes, I think I just said that, who's calling. She kept her composure now although all the clones eyes were focused on her and she was becoming nervous. I'm the person that's going to make you wish you were never born the voice said. Are you alone? She swallowed the popcorn fast. No I'm with ten fuckers who'll pop you like a cherry, want some?

Listen Lady, you're dead meat and tell your house guest she is dead too. You got it buddy, when I get myself a house guest maybe female since you said her,

I'll relay the message Ok? The caller hung up loudly in her ear. Tacy holding the receiver still in her hand dangling it looked at her clones. Ok ladies we're on. Tacy drove them to the airport in her Mercedes and rented them cars of their choices. Their was no palm she hadn't read or greased in her community.

She was calling on all her contacts that owed her favors.

All the Clones now were just that Clones. They set their watches Aunt Tacy had brought for them to make them beep at the same time. They were also packing identical pistols that shot identical bullets tucked into their waist packs that were identical and glowed' in the dark. Everything about them was the same. They took their waist packs off before they entered the bar. The glowing bags was only for protection if they could not find their pistols in the dark, in the car. God forbid if they needed their guns while in their cars, that meant the plan must have went wrong. Tacy parked her car after her Clones did and entered the bar last. They entered one after another. Tacy checked her watch as she stood in the doorway Eight o'clock. Everyone in the crowed bar knew Tacy well. She staggered, mumbling her usual bullshit, trying to sell her business while eyeballing everyone trying to spot three unlucky assholes that wanted to become hero's and wanted to fuck with her nieces. Tia entered the bar first, earlier looking like a mouse lost in a maze. She looked like an informer who came directly from the police stations library basement. She wore glasses with a short ponytail that her newly cut hair would allow her to wear and wore a long flowered dress. No patron in the bar gave her the time of night. To them she was a cop. She sat in a corner booth alone.

This part of the plan called for them not to look alike but take on different disguises before they exited their cars. Aunt Tacy stumbled and fell to the floor. Good God Tacy the bartender yelled. Are you drunk? He'd never seen Tacy drunk before, talking bullshit but never drunk. Fuck you slime ball she said loudly, I'm just getting started. She picked herself up from the floor, I'll take a scotch, a scotch, and a scotch please. She slurred holding herself up with the bar. There are three things that can be good for me tonight. And guess what? All three are scotch. She roared attracting much attention. You look like Larry Moe and Curly, ha, ha, ha. Somebody get me a chair before I fall. I'll be damn, I'm drunk, I think. She laughed again. A left over hippie from the sixty's led her to a seat. He was leathered and chained, his hair were matted long into a ponytail that reached down to the back of his belt. His chain belt caught onto Tacy's dress.

As they untangled themselves from each other she slurred. Thanks Mister, I love you. Where you been all my life? I owe you one. Bar keep give Mr. Magoo here drinks on me. What is your name anyway fellow she slurred, almost falling down again. He helped her up again and kindly placed her into the booth with Tia, the sure to be cop, thinking what a perfect match they made.

The cop and the drunk. Buy me a drink bitch she said with spit flying as the hippie walked away going back to his own party. Lady did you call me a bitch Tia said rising herself up over the drunken lady. Don't you even call me bitch, my name is Tia, Tia Morgan to be exact. Norway almost fell off his stool. Tacy gave Tia silent words looking at him then back to her. One down and two more assholes to conquer. Norway walked up to Tia completely ignoring the drunken lady. Can I sweetheart, have a minute of your time? What did you say your name was?

What it was is what it is Tia said to him, and that's what it will always be. Got a problem with that. No problem, Norway said but I can become your worst nightmare. Where the fuck is the money? Don't bother getting up, I already had your Aunt's house checked and it's not there, so you tell me where my money is and I'll let it be up to God when it's your time to stop breathing, Ok. Fuck off man you don't Know me. Norway reached into his jacket pocket above his mid body a motion like he was reaching for a hanky from his shirt pocket. He patted his chest softly, I have a gun right here lady so I suggest you follow my lead. He grabbed her by her arm.

114

Mirrored Injustice

Let's go. Tia started to wail her ass off. She held both her arms up high in the air running from the crazy man screaming as he was shot and fell short of touching her behind. Tia became hysterical running faster holding arms up towards the ceiling. Father Jessup and Mike Mehan ran over to the dying man. The drunk lady staggered among the crowd interrupting the goings on.

Someone grabbed the out of control girl that everyone took for a cop but knew differently now and stopped her before she got out of the bar. The police were called, then a doctor to pronounce the man truly dead, then the coroner arrived to take him to the nearest morgue while the police took the hysterical lady with them to the police station for farther questioning. Tia stayed there for five hours saying the same think over and over. I never saw the man before. She told them she was visiting a relative and by her driver's license they know she was from Colorado and staying with her Aunt Tacy. They Knew Tacy and it appeared a that she had no record that they could find and neither did her niece. Later after finding no cause to hold her on besides alcoholism and stupidity, they let her go having a police women drive her to her hotel room. She also told them she came for a visit with her Aunt and being in the wrong place at the wrong time. She told them that she came to Hawaii after years of saving for a vacation with her pinochle club. After her ticket was already purchased she realized her club mates didn't meet their financial duties. She decided to take the trip alone because she knew she had an Aunt that lived here. Being that her ticket was non-refundable and all.

After everything calmed down in the wee hours of the morning. Tia took a cab back to Aunt Tacys house. One down, two more to go, they toasted each other in awe. The next day the Hawaiian headlines read. Man dies in barroom brawl. An unknown assailant shoots wild man after he attacks an innocent bystander. Have vigilantes taken on the Hawaiian Police Force. Aunt Tacy and her Clones toasted again, they ate and drank themselves into oblivion. Their favorite thing to do after a good afternoon was to take a nap. After each napped to their satisfactions, they ate again and planned their next strategies. Meanwhile, Father Jessup and Mike Mehan was baffled by Norway's death and the headlines. Who would shoot Norway Woods here? Father Jessup said putting down the paper. He took a long drag on a cigarette. His entire personality had changed since he came to Hawaii. He had on cream colored creased baggie Kakis and a Hawaii shirt that he brought from one of the patrons in the bar previously. His shoes were pointy toed and black. His hat was black and pointed too, a replica of Michael Jacksons. He didn't know that because he didn't know who Michael Jackson was. He was starting to tan and his hair was getting sun blown. He smoked his cigarette up in four puffs. I don't know Mike said. Maybe it's possible that he wasn't telling us the truth. Lord only knows the Father said. Whatever the truth may be, I only hope that whoever killed him don't connect us with his death. I don't want no part of this. I've only come here for one reason. I don't want no part of this shit either Mike said I'm on a mission too. Be quiet Father said, I'm going to make a call. He picked up the phone and dialed Mother Mary's number. She picked up and he poured his soul out, telling her everything he did since he got off the plane up to Norway getting killed. I don't believe one thing have anything to do with the other she yelled at him. Find the Sister! You know I told you before you left here that she has something valuable that could put us up the creek without a paddle for a long time. She probably done xeroxed them by now, Xeroxed what? Father Jessup questioned her. George honey you know how much we've done, I don't need to sit here and listen to this ignorance from you. You know Sister Tangela was my bookkeeper as well as yours. She was the one that kept you from appointing a bookkeeper of your own, because she was so good. You've got just as much to lose as I do. Remember you were the one who had the affair with the dead Sister Bridgette Johnson, or should I remind you. Don't deny it now, we're in this too deep. We could very well be accused of the murder if we're not careful. And if you don't bring Sister Mancini back soon. So she can get just what she deserves.

I've covered up enough here on my part, I need Sister Mancini to confess to the murder, so don't hurt her, it's up to you if you want to beat the living shit out of her, if that's what gets your rocks off. Bring her to me, and remember George, don't fuck the girl. I'll know if you do, your face gives you away every time. Another thing. Forget about the dead guy. He already bagged and tagged ok honey. I'll see you when you see me, with the girl understand bye. Mary don't hang up the Father said frantically. Shit, that bitch, he slammed down the phone. Mike was pale enough without the Father adding to his problems. What's the deal man, are you staying here to do your deal or not Mike said wiping his dripping sweat. I'm staying the Father said, where do we go from here? I'm don't know, I'm not sure, Mike said, I guess we go back to the bar for starters. Father Jessup smoked his cigarettes and paced the floor. I need to find me a nun real bad. And I need to find me a slut, who's my wife Mike said interrupting the Father. I'm gonna show that bitch how a man is suppose to be treated, when I finish with her she'll be sorry she ever left California or woke up this morning.

Meanwhile back at Aunt Tacys, the Clones didn't mind being called Clones anymore. They got to know each other better than they knew themselves or the backs of their hands.

The three read each other's mind like their brains were connected. The phone rang. Tacy jumped. She talked low into the receiver. After she finished her conversation she turned to the clones and said.

Round two, everybody get ready, we're on. This plan is Mall call, you all know what to do. They did. They had rehearsed so many times they couldn't change a thing if they wanted to. To make it better. The lady who rang

Aunt Tacys phone was a longtime friend of hers, Mrs Mae. She was the owner of the hotel that the three men were staying in, minus Norway Woods. She informed Tacy that the two men would be staying there again tonight. Now Mae told Tacy they just left heading for the Mall. Mae would get a tidy sum for her information granted Tacy had already co-signed the second mortgage on Maes business. That was not spoken about now. Aunt Tacy and the Clones dressed for the occasion.

They still had their separate rented cars. The next day's paper said that the hysterical women that was involved in the barroom murder booked a flight as fast as she could out of Hawaii.

But the paper. Didn't know that a paid derelict took her seat on the plane and was glad to do so. The transient had run out of food long ago and as willing to accommodate anyone that fed her.

The Clones and Aunt Tacy positioned themselves around all the men clothing stores in the Mall. They stalked their last two lonely hero's that was trying to destroy something Tacy thought was precious. Aunt Tacy sat in the entrance with a small two way radio. Before long she spotted the two men who were bent over a coffee in the shop next to a men's clothing store. She spoke low, Ok girls I've got them in my sight, pay attention. Their getting up now and going into Stacks Hawaiian Disguise Shop. Let's nip this in the bud quick. There were no mistaking these two for anyone else according to Mae's descriptions. Each Clone including Aunt Tacy positioned themselves in different places watching the two assholes try desperately to disguise themselves. Mike went into dressing room six to try on a pair of shorts. Since his lifestyle had been to always be sheik, and wear creased silk slacks at all times he decided now to do the opposite. Trying to play down his personality a bit. He pulled his pants off and reached for the loud shorts he chose off the racks five minutes earlier that should have been on the bench beside him in the dressing room. Someone appeared and handed him his shorts. The person looked so much like his wife h e automatically tried to slap her although he wasn't sure whether it was Torese or not. It was a natural, normal reflex for him. He swung and missed, as the power in his fist was so forceful it took him down to the floor. He looked up at the person not really seeing anything, when he focused he saw two more wives of his besides the one who handed him his pants, They were coming at him from the Mirror. But there was only a mirror in front of him, no mirrors on either of his sides. He swung at one not believing what he was seeing, but deciding to fight anyway.

He reached for his gun from the old cowboy hoister still wrapped around his naked waist. One of his wives relieved him of it snatching it out of his hand while the other two smiled at him. He then reached for his pants because that's where his extra revolver was along with a knife folded up that came out a foot once the button was flicked. Another person who also looked like his wife grabbed his pants a split second before he touched them. You want these honey she waved them close enough for him to almost touch. Follow me. Like a stupid fool, he left the stall and obeyed his wife for the first time in his life. Not knowing which was his wife but following the one who said follow me.

This wife mesmerized him, as if he was in a trance and had no control over himself, he yearned for her better days. The other Clones in the mirror were just fantasies he thought now losing himself in this crazy dream. One of his fantasies yelled rape flying out of the stall with him coming out behind her. She came out of the stall and led him all the way into the crowd yelling rape before he focused on his half nude body and realized what was happening. He was in full view of the customers and the stores staff. He was bare ass to the bone from his waist down. He'd forgotten his bikini briefs had come off with his pants and he being to lazy to entangle the mess he created. Help me, help me, the wife who looked like his wife screamed. Everyone's eyes were on the man, as the lady ran with her arms flying frantically. She hit some poor old lady in the eye with her elbow. A shot rang out and her and the old lady fell to the floor for cover, it seemed to come from nowhere. It stopped the half-naked man dead in his tracks. Seconds later the store and the mall was in total chaos. Lots of people ran to the parking lot and it cleared out in no time. Police appeared everywhere. The hysterical lady who seem to be the target of the incident was totally out of control. He tried to rape me she yelled, where's my pocketbook. She dropped her pocketbook when she hit the poor old lady. I need my pocketbook she screamed. My kids pictures, my God, somebody help me Torese spent the next twenty four hours in the hands of the authorities. First at the hospital to be checked thoroughly and later the police station to bc questioned farther. At one point tie authorities thought they might have to transfer her to a psych ward. They questioned her over and over. All she said was I never saw the man before, where's my pocketbook. My Kids baby pictures are all gone, somebody please help me. She told the police that she was a runaway but refused to tell them where she'd ran away from.

She said she was only in the store to kill time because she had nowhere to go. She also said men would continue to rape her if she told them where she lived. As they insisted that she must tell them where she lived she became hysterical all over again. They sent a female social worker to calm her down without any luck. The girl's purse was gone and so was her identification. Meanwhile at the mall they had little clues to go on.

The missing purse had never turned up and they realized that it could very well never turn up giving someone the opportunity to be richer they were when they awakened that morning.

The dead man and his belongings were taken to the morgue. It was decided that neither gun they confiscated was the murder weapon.

They were baffled by the crime and on top of that they had to deal with this crazy lady who told them that the man pulled her into the dressing room at gun point and tried to rape her. And she was incoherent. At one point they thought she didn't know her name. Every time she was asked her name, she responded with the same answer. The man is going to rape me. And I can't tell you where I live because I have no home, I can't tell you my name because I have none. They took her back to the hospital to the mental ward anyway and locked her up in a secure room for the night after she was psychiatrically evaluated. The next morning, she wasn't in the room or the ward when the doors were opened. The paper read. Man shot to death at a local Mall while trying to assault an unknown woman. Anyone with the whereabouts of this women should call the Hawaiian Police Department. They gave her description of between eighteen to twenty, with blond hair that hung to her waist in a ponytail, wearing shorts and a halter top.

They ended the story with bold letters. IS THERE A VIGILANTE IN KAHO'OLAWE HAWAII? The Clones toasted with much food and drink.

Father Jessup phoned Mother Mary. He was pale and distraught after seeing Mike get shot in the Mall half naked. I'm getting the hell out of here, don't tell me about no fucking coincidences. If you want the girl so bad then you'll have to come and get her yourself. You do the job, I'm catching the next thing smoking out of here. With that the holy

Father who ran the Monastery short of two years from becoming the Abbot slammed the phone down. He started to pack. He was so nervous he decided that his clothes were not as important as his life. He stopped all

his packing activity and headed for the door. When he
opened it, there stood two police officers who were
similar to the television show Hawaii Five. They had on
sleeveless shirts, loud shorts, and sandals. The only way
to tell they were police officers was by the hoisters and
garb carried on their waist. George Jessup you are under
arrest for the murders of Norway Woods and Mike
Mehan. You have the right to remain silent. You have
the right to an attorney, if you cannot afford an attorney.
The officer took a deep breath, One will be appointed for
you. Come with us. Father Jessup shook uncontrollable
and stared to cry. He couldn't speak as the officers
turned him around and handcuffed him. Other higher
uppers and newspaper journalists started to arrive while
they walked him out of the hotel. Everything was
captured on camera which made the evening news.
They took him away on a motorized cart, how
Hawaiian. The Police Sergeant in charge told the
reporters that he thought the vigilante had indeed been
caught.

They searched and fingerprinted Father Jessup's
hotel room, retrieving weapons that could have been
responsible for the two unexplained murders. The
authorities also found a suitcase containing over a
million dollars. Now they had a suspect and a motive.
An anonymous person called also and said that a certain
Mother Mary from Philadelphia was the Grand wizard

behind the two crimes. This person told the Police that Mother Mary hired three men to kill a nun to cover up a murder that happened at her convent. They then faxed contents to the station containing evidence at the convent that the arrested man and Mother Mary were lovers and partners in crime.

The fax revealed lots of embezzlement facts that the two were into, enough in fact to put them behind bars for a long time.

Father Jessup plead guilty to murder and embezzlement waving his rights to a jury trial. He chooses to be sentenced by a Judge because if he had chosen a jury and been found guilty he could have indeed been sentenced to his death. He was sentenced to life instead, without the chance of parole. Attempted rape was added and later rape because of all the orphaned children that was his prey for the last thirty years or more. Mother Mary was either aware of the goings on or she may have participated in it and covered it up for years. The two girls that was involved in the incidents, one was murdered and one got away only to return to testify against the two culprits. Mother Mary and Father Jessup had a hard time adjusting their eyes and thoughts when they saw the good Sister whom they raised practically as their adopted daughter.

They raised her to be so earthly and pure. She looked like their girl yet she was now cultured and strong. Now there were three images of her, they only thought they recognized the one that was to testify against them. In the hall, they weren't sure who either girl was. And as they thought their eyes were playing tricks on them all together. They never told anyone of the clones they thought they saw in the halls. Mother Mary received Fifteen years and Father Jessup got life.

Tia didn't return to Aspen for a long time. She called her parents often reassuring them that she was ok. Her parents never fully understood what finally made her grow up enough to venture out on her own, leaving Aspen in her past. They were scared, so they didn't mention her lifestyle. Tia found herself on her own without making them out to be the bad guys. Every time she talked to them, she would end the conversation by saying, I'll be home soon, maybe. I love you, tell Grands I love her too. She eventually bought a Tavern on the most occupied beach on the island, with her parents and Aunt Tacy's help. She grew that year like a wild Roses.

It took a lot of time for Tia to understand and like herself. Understanding herself only made her more adult like, as she learned to like herself. Being a lady was what she always wanted to be. Before. Now and forever.

Torese Mehan did very well without the psychological and physical abuse and the influence that Mike forced on her for so many years. She adjusted well missing her children until her baby Mitchell was in her arms at last. Reese eventually moved her three children to Hawaii after a year of them living with her parents after their Dad suddenly died not long after their Mother had disappeared. She telephoned her parents often, insuring them that she was ok with each call. Again as the loving parents they were they didn't question her motives, loving her enough to be happy for her that she finally had gotten away and out of a bad situation. She told her children that she loved them very much over and over again once she had them in her arms and surrounded them with the warmth of her body. She explained to the older two how their dad suddenly died. Her goal in her life now was to make up for all the wrong doings that Mike had inflicted on her offspring as she tried to make her older two twins love and respect her as she loved and cherished them. The year before she got her children back she attended the police academy of Hawaii and now she was a Kaho'olawe police officer. She kept in touch with her parents that raised her, but it was no big deal to her anymore, only out of respect. She felt out of place with them all her life and she never went home again. Now she was finally home and she wanted to be the best Police officer and Mother that she could possibly be.

Tangela (Tandy) Mancini earned her teaching certificate that same year. Helping with first grade children in Hawaii's finest first grade private school. She was still the sane person that knocked on Aunt Tacy's door late into the night. Now she had a different point of view about her life.

Mother Mary and father Jessup were prisoned long before. During Tandy's last year in Hawaii she earned a teaching Certificate at the local Community College while working with first grade children in a private school name Hawaiian Rose.

She continued her education at night while she taught children during the day. She fell in love slowly with the school's principle. He returned her feelings tit for tat.

She was adjusted and happy with her new life as long as she kept in close contact with her new family.

Aunt Tacy often had all the Clones and Reese's children over for food and drinks. She'd given them all a place in her life and a place in her home until each of them got on their feet. They respected her and she loved and respected them each as individuals. She had long ago stopped calling them her Clones, but she was tempted every time she looked at one of her three nieces. She learned to love them for the great humans they were individually. She now recognized whom from who as soon as her eyes focused on their faces. She liked their personalities as people and they adored her. Aunt Tacy always thought what goes around eventually comes back at people. Now she was at her happiest as God, faith and fate brought her three only family members her way.

They all had their own lives now and Aunt Tacy was a part of that in every way.

One particular evening while they all toasted grill cheeses for the kids and chicken and salad for the adults, along with their loving partners who they thought was important enough to bring along after a hard day's work. The doorbell rang.

Aunt Tacy excused herself to answer the door. She became white as a ghost. Her three nieces automatically knew something was wrong as they had come to know her well in these last years. They hadn't seen her stuttering in a long time. Not since the clones and Tacy troubles had been finalized.

Girls we have company, please come into the parlor with me, leave the children and your company where they are. This is a family matter she stuttered. Follow me please. They each rose instantly. Aunt Tact never said please anymore once she gotten to know them, unless it was to please herself. They obeyed like clockwork. The best way to handle their Aunt Tacy was to not ask her questions when she made a statement. It was better to obey and listen then to doubt what was on her mind. They each followed her through the living room and into the parlor.

Mirrored Injustice

Reaching the parlor, they stared speechless, then looked at each other for comfort. There were two more perfect identical female Clones standing there looking more frighten then wet cats. There was also a third person with them. Their translator. These two new Clones spoke no English.

But they knew exactly what they were looking for and whom. They were so identical to the three Clones. Aunt Tacy cried as she took the initiative to introduce everybody.

About The Author

Cookie Johnson Grant spent her first 25 years in North Philadelphia. Then her next 20 years in Aspen Colorado. She now resides in Aurora Colorado.

www.ingramcontent.com/pod-product-compliance
Lightning Source LLC
Chambersburg PA
CBHW071029280326
41935CB00011B/1509